50 RECIPES FOR

COLOURFUL HANGING BASKETS

50 RECIPES FOR

COLOURFUL HANGING BASKETS

RICHARD BIRD

WARD LOCK

A WARD LOCK BOOK

First published in the UK 1997 by Ward Lock
Wellington House, 125 Strand
London WC2R 0BB

A Cassell Imprint

Distributed in the United States
by Sterling Publishing Co., Inc.
387 Park Avenue South, New York, NY 10016–8810

Distributed in Canada
by Cavendish Books Inc.
Unit 5, 801 West 1st Street
North Vancouver, B.C., Canada V7P 1PH

A British Library Cataloguing in Publication Data block for this book
may be obtained from the British Library

ISBN 0 7063 7557 2

Designed by Richard Carr
Printed and bound in Spain

Contents

Introduction

COULD THERE BE a better way of brightening up the front of a house or cheering up a boring garage than a hanging basket teeming with colour? Here are 50 recipes to give you some ideas for livening up your own home and garden. You will find baskets to suit all moods and situations, ranging from simple, elegant arrangements to frothy extravaganzas – something for everyone, in fact.

A colourful basket made up from ingredients that are readily available from any garden centre.

Hanging baskets are a simple way of extending your garden. Because they allow you to move upwards and across buildings, walls, fences and posts, they enable you to introduce an extra dimension to your garden. The intensive care that they are given in terms of regular watering and feeding means that hanging baskets become concentrated balls of flower power, so you can cram far more plants into a small area than you can in a traditional bed or border.

Baskets also allow you to change the character of your house and garden. What could be a rather bland, uninteresting façade can be transformed by a colourful basket, and if you tire of the arrangement, it is a simple matter to replace or remove it altogether. Hanging baskets are a simple and inexpensive way of making changes – certainly less costly and time consuming than repainting your house – to match your mood or the season. The plants and baskets themselves are relatively cheap and widely available, and it requires little in the way of gardening expertise to put on a very effective display.

It is not only the buildings and walls that they adorn that are cheered up by baskets. The gardeners who create them also get a thrill every time they look at their handiwork. The sight of a colourful basket is enough to lift anyone's spirits, but to know that you have produced the display yourself is doubly satisfying. Not all would-be gardeners have a garden in which they can practise their art but most can find space to hang at least one basket. Even those people with vast gardens still derive great pleasure from creating these small patches of colour and delight. It is not only the creators who feel pleasure in their creations, of course. Even the most hardened office-bound commuters will be cheered as they walk along a street brightened by baskets overflowing with flowers and foliage.

While one tends to think of hanging baskets as cheerful and colourful, this does not mean that they need be garish. There is a tremendous range of possible styles, from the outright vulgar – and why not occasionally splash out? – to the quiet and the sophisticated.

Hanging baskets are cheap to buy and to fill. There are different styles available, but even the most expensive will not break the bank. The plants are reasonably cheap to buy, and if you have the time and space you can always raise your own from seeds or cuttings, perhaps sharing the expense and the resulting plants with a friend or neighbour. All the materials you are likely to want are available from garden centres or nurseries, and they can be bought in comparatively small quantities so that you will not have to store huge bags of compost or fertilizer, which can be a problem if you do not have a garden.

Many newcomers to hanging-basket gardening do not have the time or the skill to create their own designs and to experiment with different combinations of plants. It is hoped that this book will provide a starting point. In it you will find 50 different recipes for creating a successful display. If you do not have much experience of planting up a hanging basket, just follow these suggestions and you will find that it is relatively easy to achieve satisfying results. After you have prepared a few, you will soon want to experiment for yourself and will start to create your own designs. At first these may be simple variations on one of the recipes in the book, but gradually you will acquire the confidence to branch out on your own, choosing your own plants and the ways you use them.

In this book, each of the recipes contains enough information to produce a hanging basket similar to the one illustrated. You will find details of the ingredients you will require, including the types of plants and the way to plant them. However, it should be remembered that none of these recipes is sacrosanct. You should feel free to make any modifications that you wish – for example, you may not like a particular plant or it may not be available in your local garden centre or nursery. The plants listed are only suggestions, and there are usually plenty of similar alternatives that you can obtain. Modify the basket as much as you like, and remember that if you do not succeed, you can always take it apart and make another!

Hanging baskets can be used in a wide variety of places. Here an attractive example hangs within a wooden pergola.

Spring Time

*H*ANGING BASKETS ARE *often left in the shed or greenhouse until it is time to plant up the summer bedding, but they can be used at any time of year. Spring arrangements are particularly welcome, and daffodils and snowdrops will always brighten the dull days of early spring. This basket can be prepared in autumn or the bulbs can be grown in pots and planted up just before the basket is put on display. You could use other spring bulbs to create any number of variations on this theme.*

INGREDIENTS

10 miniature daffodils (*Narcissus* 'Tête-à-Tête') **(A)**
36 double snowdrops (*Galanthus nivalis* 'Flore Pleno') **(B)**
6 variegated ivies (*Hedera helix*) **(C)**

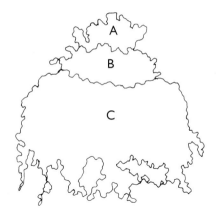

CONTAINER

30cm (12in) plastic-covered wire container

MATERIALS

Liner
Branches of Lawson's cypress or other conifer
General-purpose compost

POSITION

Any site out of a cold wind.

PLANTING

1. So that the flowering times coincide, it is best to grow the different ingredients in pots and to use a substitute bulb – muscari, for example – if the daffodils and snowdrops are not in flower at the same time. Plant up just before display.

2. Rest the basket on a bucket to make it easier to work, and line the inside with small twigs of conifer. Carefully place the liner on the bed of twigs.

3. Place the daffodils in the centre of the basket, either still in the pot or as a solid lump, and filter the compost under and around them. Arrange the snowdrops around this central feature, taking care not to disturb the roots when you take them from their pots. Pack the compost firmly around them. Finally, ease the ivies around the rim of the basket without disturbing the bulbs.

4. Level off the compost, firming it down so that the final level is about 2.5cm (1in) below the rim of the basket.

5. Stand the basket in a bucket of water to give the contents a good soak.

MAINTENANCE

Once soaked, this basket should not need a great deal of watering as long as the compost is kept just damp, although if it is in a sunny or windy position it could dry out very rapidly. Remove the basket as soon as the bulbs begin to fade.

Spring Posy

THE FIRST PRIMROSES and polyanthus are always a welcome sign that spring is just around the corner and that summer is not far behind. This bright basket is easy to prepare because all the primroses are grown in separate pots and assembled when they are in flower. This makes substitution easy should any of the plants run out of flower power. Because none of the flowers trails over the edge, the basket's liner will show, so you should either cover it with leaves or use moss.

INGREDIENTS

12 pots of mixed coloured primroses (*Primula*) **(A)**

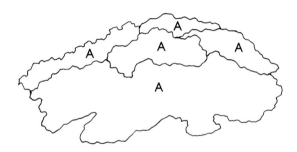

CONTAINER

30cm (12in) plastic-covered wire container

MATERIALS

Liner
Some branches of Lawson's cypress or other conifer
General-purpose compost

POSITION

Sunny to semi-shaded position.

PLANTING

1. This basket can be prepared in the autumn but is best left until the primroses come into flower so that you can select those that will be in flower at the same time and use the colours you prefer.

2. Place the basket in a bucket to hold it steady while you work, then line it with conifer twigs so that the liner of the basket will not be seen. Alternatively, line the basket with moist sphagnum moss.

3. Fill the basket to the rim with the compost and gently firm it down.

4. Buy or grow about 20 primulas so that you have a choice of colours and flowering times when you make up the basket. Select those that you want, water them and leave for a while to take up the moisture. Remove them from their pots and plant without disturbing the root balls.

5. Firm down the compost around the plants and level off the surface to about 2.5cm (1in) below the edge of the basket.

6. Water thoroughly by standing the basket in a bucket of water.

MAINTENANCE

Because this is a spring display it will not need as much water as a summer display, particularly if the weather is showery. However, sunny, hot spells can suddenly dry out the compost, and if the primulas wilt, water them immediately. If a plant stops flowering, replace it with a fresh pot. When the basket is finished, plant the primroses in the garden.

Pink Cascade

*T*HIS IS A SPECTACULAR *wall basket, which is made from quite common ingredients but which creates a sophisticated effect. The colours, mainly pinks, go together well, and the touch of blue of the felicia provides a subtle contrast, while the grey helichrysums make a sympathetic background. Although nearly all the flowers are pink, there is a great variation in their shapes and textures so the whole scheme is far from boring. The size and smooth petals of the petunias make them the focal point of the display.*

INGREDIENTS

2 pink petunias (*Petunia* 'Trailing Pink') **(A)**
2 pink lobelias (*Lobelia* 'Lilac Cascade') **(B)**
2 Swan River daisies (*Brachycome iberidifolia* 'Blue Star') **(C)**
2 double ivy-leaved geraniums (*Pelargonium* 'Galilee') **(D)**
1 busy lizzie (*Impatiens*) **(E)**
1 blue felicia (*Felicia amelloides*) **(F)**
2 helichrysums (*Helichrysum petiolare*) **(G)**
1 pink verbena (*Verbena* 'Sissinghurst') **(H)**
1 fuchsia (*Fuchsia* 'Flirtation Waltz') **(I)**

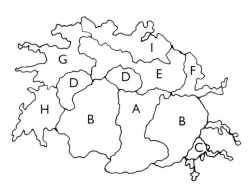

CONTAINER

45cm (18in) half-basket

MATERIALS

Liner
General-purpose compost
Water-retaining granules
Slow-release fertilizer tablet or granules

POSITION

A sunny position is required, preferably protected from wind.

PLANTING

1. Plant up in early summer. The basket can be planted in spring if it is kept under glass until frosts have passed.

2. If possible, hang this basket on a wall while you fill it to make your work easier. Put a liner in the basket.

3. Part fill the container with a general-purpose compost and mix in some water-retaining granules. If you wish, mix in fertilizer granules at this stage, too.

4. Make holes in the side of the liner and plant the verbena and one each of the petunias, Swan River daisies and lobelias. If you have used a waterproof liner, these plants will have to be added to the top of the basket. Continue to add compost, gently firming it down as you work.

5. Plant the rest of the basket, starting with the other petunia and the geraniums and then fitting the other plants around them. Be careful with the brittle stems of the petunias.

6. Firm down the compost between the plants and level it off at about 2.5cm (1in) below the rim of the basket. Water.

MAINTENANCE

Keep well watered. If you did not use a slow-release fertilizer, add a liquid feed to the water once a week.

Cool Summer

*T*HIS DISPLAY IS *guaranteed to cool down even the hottest summer. The white of the petunias and lobelia blends perfectly with the pale green, yellow-splashed leaves, while the yellow of the begonia also adds to the effect. The orange-red of the cupheas brings a subtle touch of colour, but even their variegated leaves contribute to the overall yellow and white theme. The choice of background is important – the sympathetic colour of this mellow sandstone is perfect.*

INGREDIENTS

2 white petunias (*Petunia* 'Trailing White') **(A)**
3 variegated cupheas (*Cuphea ignea* 'Variegata') **(B)**
2 variegated pick-a-back plants (*Tolmiea menziesii* 'Taff's Gold') **(C)**
1 white lobelia (*Lobelia* 'White Cascade') **(D)**
1 yellow begonia (*Begonia* × *tuberhybrida* 'Gold Cascade') **(E)**

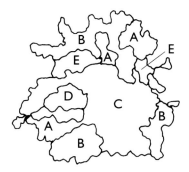

CONTAINER

30cm (12in) plastic-covered wire container

MATERIALS

Liner
Lime-free (ericaceous) compost
Water-retaining granules
Slow-release fertilizer tablet or granules

POSITION

Sunny to semi-shaded position.

PLANTING

1. Prepare the display in early summer or in spring if it can be kept under glass until the frosts have finished.

2. Place the basket on a bucket to make it easier to handle. Put the liner in place and trim if necessary.

3. Three-quarters fill the basket with compost, using a lime-free mix because begonias like acid conditions. Add the water-retaining and, if used, fertilizer granules and mix well into the compost. Continue to fill the basket, gently pressing down the compost as you work.

4. Start by positioning the begonia, taking care not to damage it when you insert the other plants. Next plant the pick-a-back plants, and then the petunias. Carefully tuck in the rest of the plants.

5. Firm down the compost around the plants and level off the surface to about 2.5cm (1in) below the rim of the basket. If you did not use granules, press a fertilizer tablet into the compost.

6. Place the basket in a bucket of water to give it a thorough soaking.

MAINTENANCE

Even though there are water-retaining granules in the compost, it will need regular watering, especially in hot weather. If you have not used a slow-release fertilizer, add a liquid feed to the water once a week. Deadhead to keep the display looking fresh, and trim off any wayward shoots.

Summer Heat

*T*HERE IS A TENDENCY *to think of brightly coloured plants as those that grow in the sun, but there are a few that will grow in the shade. Begonias are good examples of plants that prefer to be out of the sun's hot rays, and yet many have strongly coloured flowers. The rich orange of this begonia is perfectly set off by its own dark green leaves and by the pyracantha on the wall behind. The deep pink of the busy lizzie is not particularly sympathetic with the overall scheme, and you might prefer to use a different colour.*

INGREDIENTS

1 orange begonia (*Begonia* × *tuberhybrida* 'Orange Cascade') **(A)**
1 pink busy lizzie (*Impatiens*) **(B)**
2 blue lobelias (*Lobelia* 'Blue Cascade') **(C)**
2 red lobelias (*Lobelia* 'Ruby Cascade') **(D)**

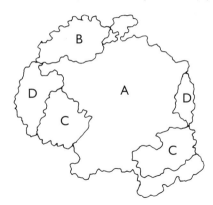

CONTAINER

25cm (10in) half-basket

MATERIALS

Liner
Lime-free (ericaceous) compost
Water-retaining granules
Slow-release fertilizer tablet or granules

POSITION

Place against a wall that does not get the hot midday sun.

PLANTING

1. Make up the basket at the beginning of summer, once the frosts have passed. If kept under glass, it can be made up in advance so that it is in full flower when it is moved into the open.

2. Temporarily hang the basket on a wall or support it on a bucket while you work. Place a liner in the basket, using a waterproof one if you are worried about staining the wall.

3. Three-quarters fill the basket with compost and then add the water-retaining granules. Stir well so that they are thoroughly mixed in. If you wish, mix in fertilizer granules, too. Finish filling the basket and press down the compost lightly.

4. Plant the begonia in the centre of the basket. Plant the busy lizzie behind and to one side of the begonia so that it is not too dominant. Next plant the lobelias, tucking them under the foliage of the other two plants.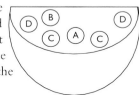

5. Gently firm down the compost between the plants and level off the surface of the compost so that it is about 2.5cm (1in) below the rim of the basket. Press a fertilizer tablet into the compost if you have not already used granules. Water thoroughly.

MAINTENANCE

Do not allow the basket to dry out. If you have used a slow-release fertilizer, there is no need to add a liquid feed. Remove dead flowers as they appear.

The Hanging Gardens

*T*HE BEAUTY OF *this basket lies in the choice of foliage. The central feature is the wonderful cascade of variegated ground ivy. The bronze leaves of the fittonia contrast well with this and at the same time work well with the pinks of the fuchsias and the busy lizzie. Tucked in to one side is a pick-a-back plant, which continues the variegated theme of the ground ivy. This is a full basket, which will keep its good looks over a long period.*

INGREDIENTS

1 fittonia (*Fittonia albivenis* 'Verschaffeltii') **(A)**
1 pink busy lizzie (*Impatiens*) **(B)**
2 pink fuchsias (*Fuchsia* 'Mrs Popple') **(C)**
1 variegated pick-a-back plant (*Tolmiea menziesii* 'Taff's Gold') **(D)**
2 variegated ground ivies (*Glechoma hederacea* 'Variegata') **(E)**

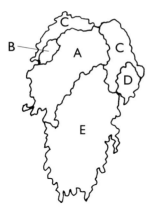

CONTAINER

30cm (12in) plastic-covered wire container

MATERIALS

Liner
General-purpose compost
Water-retaining granules
Slow-release fertilizer tablet or granules

POSITION

This display needs to be in a sunny position and must be protected from winds and draughts.

PLANTING

1. Make up the basket in early summer once frosts have passed. Alternatively, to get it growing well, prepare it in spring and keep it in a conservatory or greenhouse

2. It is easier to work with the basket held in a bucket, but if the basket ivies are already trailing, hang up.

3. Line the basket and three-quarters fill it with a general-purpose compost. Mix into this the water-retaining granules. If you are using slow-release fertilizer granules, add these at this stage too.

4. Plant the ivies at the front of the basket and take care not to break the stems as you add the other plants. Insert the creeping fittonia in the centre and behind this place the two fuchsias. Finally, tuck in the pick-a-back plant and the busy lizzie on either side.

5. If you can get between the plants, firm down the compost gently, finishing it off about 2.5cm (1in) below the level of the rim. If used, add the fertilizer tablet, then water.

MAINTENANCE

There is no need to feed if you have used granules or a tablet, but the contents must be kept watered. Keep the display tidy.

On the Wild Side

*T*HIS WONDERFUL DISPLAY *is very light and airy, and the plants form a cloud, rather like unkempt hair. Earlier in the season it will have been more compact. No single plant is a solid mass that draws the eye, and if anything, it is the pale yellow of the petunias that stands out. As a display, there is a bit of everything in it, and you could easily add some plants from your own garden – a geranium, lobelia or verbena, for example.*

INGREDIENTS

2 pale yellow petunias (*Petunia* 'Yellow Cascade') (A)
1 silver senecio (*Senecio cinerea*) (B)
2 bidens (*Bidens* 'Golden Goddess') (C)
2 pink busy lizzies (*Impatiens*) (D)
1 yellow calceolaria (*Calceolaria* 'Goldcrest') (E)
1 alonsoa (*Alonsoa* 'Scarlet Bedder') (F)
1 pink fuchsia (*Fuchsia* 'Mrs Popple') (G)
1 nasturtium (*Tropaeolum majus*) (H)
1 trailing ivy (*Hedera helix*) (I)

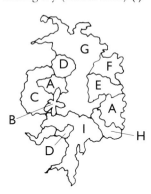

CONTAINER

35cm (14in) half-basket

MATERIALS

Liner
General-purpose compost
Water-retaining granules
Slow-release fertilizer tablet or granules

POSITION

This display needs to be in a sunny place.

PLANTING

1. Prepare this in early summer, after the frosts.

2. Hang the basket on a wall at a workable height or prop it up firmly on a table. Place a liner in the basket.

3. Three-quarters fill the basket with compost mixed with water-retaining granules and, if you are using them, fertilizer granules.

4. Make some holes in the liner and plant one of the busy lizzies, the ivy and the nasturtium. Fill the remainder of the basket and make further holes in the side to take the two bidens and the senecio.

5. Firm down the compost and then plant the top. Place the fuchsia at the centre back with the alonsoa and the other busy lizzie on either side. Put the two petunias towards the front and the calceolaria to the left.

6. Gently press down the compost around the plants and level it off to about 2.5cm (1in) below the rim of the basket. Push in a fertilizer tablet if you are using one. Water well.

MAINTENANCE

This is a full basket and will need regular watering. There is no need to feed. Remove dead flowers and stems as they appear.

Pretty Petunias

PETUNIAS ARE AMONG the aristocrats of summer bedding. Their strong yet soft shapes and rich colours make them ideal for any number of arrangements, including hanging baskets. Modern varieties are more resistant to rain and will continue to flower over a long period. Some are much more trailing in habit than previous strains, making them perfect for baskets. Dominant in this scheme are the rich purple plants, which have been lightened by a river of white and pink to one side.

INGREDIENTS

3 purple petunias (*Petunia* 'Purple Wave') **(A)**
1 pink petunia (*Petunia* 'Pastel Pink') **(B)**
1 white petunia (*Petunia* 'Trailing White') **(C)**

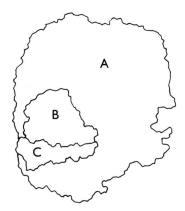

CONTAINER

35cm (14in) plastic-covered wire container

MATERIALS

Liner
General-purpose compost
Water-retaining granules
Slow-release fertilizer tablet or granules

POSITION

Hang in a sunny place, away from strong winds or draughts.

PLANTING

1. Petunias are frost tender, so do not plant them out until early summer. If you want to ensure that they are in flower when you hang out the basket, plant it up earlier but keep it in a conservatory or greenhouse.

2. If the plants are not too advanced, stand the basket in a bucket or hang it at a convenient height while you work. Line the basket with your preferred liner.

3. Three-quarters fill the basket with a general-purpose compost and mix in some water-retaining granules. If you are using fertilizer granules, mix them in now, too. Continue to fill the basket and gently press down the compost.

4. Starting at the back, plant the purple petunias, followed by the pink and white ones. Be careful not to break the brittle stalks and arrange the trailing stems as you work.

5. Carefully firm down the compost around the plants and push the fertilizer tablet into the compost if you are using one.

6. Water thoroughly. Use a bucket for small plants or a watering can if the plants are already trailing.

MAINTENANCE

In spite of the water-retaining granules the basket will need regular watering – daily in hot weather. If you have not used a slow-release fertilizer, add a liquid feed to one watering a week. Deadhead to keep the display looking its best.

Flaming Orange

*N*ASTURTIUMS ARE IDEAL *plants for hanging baskets: not only do they trail, creating the perfect shape for a basket, but they also last for a long period, giving colour right through summer and well into autumn. The variegation on the leaves of this particular variety adds a great deal of interest to the display, and the variety has the additional advantage that the flowers stand up well and are not obscured by the foliage. The lobelias, peeping out from below, are a pretty contrast.*

INGREDIENTS

3 variegated nasturtiums (*Tropaeolum majus* 'Alaska Mixed') **(A)**
2 lobelias (*Lobelia* 'Sapphire') **(B)**

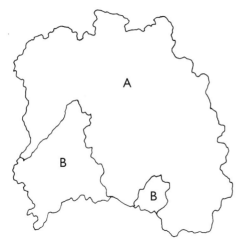

CONTAINER

30cm (12in) half-basket

MATERIALS

Liner
General-purpose compost
Water-retaining granules
Slow-release fertilizer tablet or granules

POSITION

Ideally, hang in a sunny position, although semi-shade will do.

PLANTING

1. To avoid problems with late frosts, do not start planting until early summer. For an earlier display, plant up the basket in mid-spring and keep it safely in a greenhouse or conservatory.

2. Fix the basket to a wall at a convenient height for working or, if the plants are not yet trailing, prop it up on a table. If you do not want water to drip down the wall use a water-proof liner; otherwise, line the basket as usual.

3. Three-quarters fill the basket with a general-purpose compost. Add water-retaining granules and mix well. If you are using fertilizer granules, mix these in at the same time. Continue to fill the basket and then gently firm the compost down.

4. Start the planting at the back and work your way forwards, beginning with the nasturtiums and leaving the lobelias until last.

5. Gently press down the compost and level off the surface at about 2.5cm (1in) below the rim of the basket. Press a slow-release fertilizer tablet into the compost if you wish.

6. If the plants are not trailing, place the basket in a bucket of water to soak. Otherwise, water thoroughly with a water-ing can.

MAINTENANCE

Water regularly, but there is no need to feed if you have used slow-release fertilizers. Deadhead as necessary.

Mixed Collection

*T*HIS COLOURFUL BASKET *is dominated by the large splash of blue in the centre, where the lobelia forms a focal point around which everything else is displayed. The brightness of their flowers allows the yellow bidens and begonia to stand out in the shade of the porch, while the pinks and purples of the other flowers are linked by the horizontal stripe of the light green helichrysum. If it is well cared for, this should be a long-lived display, although with time it may become a bit loose and straggly.*

INGREDIENTS

1 yellow begonia (*Begonia × tuberhybrida* 'Golden Cascade') **(A)**
2 blue lobelias (*Lobelia* 'Sapphire') **(B)**
1 blue upright petunia (*Petunia* 'Lavender') **(C)**
1 purple trailing petunia (*Petunia* 'Purple Wave') **(D)**
4 bidens (*Bidens* 'Golden Goddess') **(E)**
2 busy lizzies (*Impatiens*) **(F)**
1 limelight helichrysum (*Helichrysum petiolare* 'Limelight') **(G)**
1 ivy-leaved geranium (*Pelargonium* 'Valentine') **(H)**
1 fuchsia (*Fuchsia* 'Snowcap') **(I)**

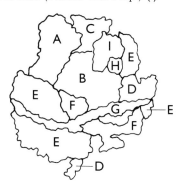

CONTAINER

35cm (14in) plastic-covered wire container

MATERIALS

Liner
Lime-free (ericaceous) compost
Water-retaining granules
Slow-release fertilizer tablet or granules

POSITION

Hang in a sunny to semi-shaded position.

PLANTING

1. This display should not be brought out into the open before early summer. It can be prepared then or planted earlier and kept under glass.

2. Either hang the basket at a working height or balance it on a bucket while you work. Place a liner inside the basket.

3. Three-quarters fill the basket with a lime-free potting compost and add the water-retaining granules. Mix well. If you want to use fertilizer granules, add these at the same time.

4. Plant two bidens, one busy lizzie and the helichrysum into the side of the basket through holes or slits in the liner.

5. Fill up the basket with compost and plant the rest of the plants, starting with the begonia, the blue petunia, the fuchsia and the geranium. Plant the other bidens and the purple petunia, set the other busy lizzie close to the front and fill in with the blue lobelia.

6. If you can manage, firm down the compost around the plants and, if used, insert the fertilizer tablet. Water well.

MAINTENANCE

Water regularly, at least once a day. There is no need to feed, but old flowers should be removed.

Bridal Wreath

W*HITE FLOWERS CONVEY not only a feeling of purity and innocence but also a great sense of tranquillity. Peace in the garden is a valuable commodity, and anything that helps to promote it should be encouraged; hanging baskets that contain predominantly white flowers are one of the methods we can use. The white petunias in this basket are echoed by the smaller lobelias. Both are set off by the subtly variegated leaves of the pick-a-back plants and the soft yellow of the begonia.*

INGREDIENTS

1 yellow begonia (*Begonia* × *tuberhybrida* 'Golden Goddess') **(A)**
4 white petunias (*Petunia* 'Falcon White') **(B)**
3 variegated pick-a-back plants (*Tolmiea menziesii* 'Taff's Gold') **(C)**
6 white lobelias (*Lobelia* 'White Cascade) **(D)**

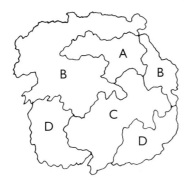

CONTAINER

30cm (12in) plastic-covered wire basket

MATERIALS

Liner
Lime-free (ericaceous) compost
Water-retaining granules
Slow-release fertilizer tablet or granules

POSITION

This basket can be in either a sunny position or one that gets sun for only part of the day. Protect from strong winds.

PLANTING

1. The best time for planting this basket is in early summer, after the threat of frosts has passed. Alternatively, it can be assembled in spring and kept hanging in shelter until needed.

2. Stand the basket in a bucket or hang it at a convenient height while you work. Place the liner in the basket.

3. Begonias need an acid soil, so use a lime-free compost. Three-quarters fill the basket with the compost and mix in the water-retaining granules together with the fertilizer granules, if you are using them.

4. Make holes in the sides of the liner and plant the six trailing lobelias through them into the compost. Continue to fill the basket, gently pressing the compost down. Plant up the basket, starting with the begonia, and then inserting the three petunias and, finally, the pick-a-back plants.

5. Firm down the compost around the plants and level off the surface to about 2.5cm (1in) below the rim of the basket. Press the fertilizer tablet, if you are using one, into the compost. Water thoroughly.

MAINTENANCE

Although there are water-retaining granules in the compost, the basket requires regular watering, especially in hot weather. However, there is no need to feed if you have used a slow-release fertilizer. Remove dead flowers as soon as they appear.

Flower Power

*T*HIS IS A *basket full of flower power, and the myriad of small lobelia flowers enhances this impression, creating as they do a haze of colour against which the other flowers are seen. The white petunias in the centre of the display immediately catch the eye, but it is the reds of the geraniums and busy lizzie on which the eye finally comes to rest. The colours are not entirely sympathetic – the orange-reds clash some-what with the pinks – but it all adds up to a colourful display, which is all that is asked of the basket.*

INGREDIENTS

1 white petunia (*Petunia* 'Falcon White') **(A)**
4 mixed lobelias (*Lobelia* 'Cascade Mixed') **(B)**
1 crimson ivy-leaved geranium (*Pelargonium* 'Regina') **(C)**
1 orange-red busy lizzie (*Impatiens*) **(D)**
2 fuchsias (*Fuchsia* 'Arabella') **(E)**
1 blue petunia (*Petunia* 'Violet') **(F)**
1 helichrysum (*Helichrysum petiolare*) **(G)**
1 scarlet ivy-leaved geranium (*Pelargonium* 'Yale') **(H)**

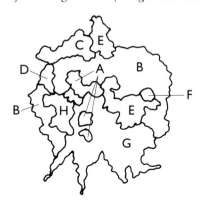

CONTAINER

35cm (14in) plastic-covered wire basket

MATERIALS

Liner
General-purpose compost
Water-retaining granules
Slow-release fertilizer tablet or granules

POSITION

Hang the basket in sun or semi-shade.

PLANTING

1. Like so many summer baskets, this is frost-tender and should not be placed outside until after the last frosts.

2. Hang the basket at a convenient working height or stand it in a bucket for ease of handling. Place the liner in the basket.

3. Pour a general-purpose compost into the basket until it is about three-quarters full and then add the water-retaining granules. If you want to use fertilizer granules, now is the time to add these. Mix well together.

4. Make holes through the liner and plant two pink lobelias and the grey-leaved helichrysum through them. Continue to fill the basket with compost and firm down.

5. Plant the surface of the basket next, starting with the petunias, fuchsias and the geraniums. Add the busy lizzie and finally tuck in the remaining lobelias.

6. Gently firm the compost and level off. Push the fertilizer tablet into the compost if you are using one. Water well.

MAINTENANCE

Water regularly, but there is no need to feed. Keep the basket tidy by deadheading.

Bright as a Button

*T*HIS IS A *perfect basket and one that most gardeners would be proud of. Although the colours are bright, they do not clash but blend together perfectly in a way that is not always easy to achieve. The careful choice of both plants and the position of the basket has produced a delight for the eye. The yellow of the pansies against their green background is an appealing contrast to the pinks and purples, but it is not just the colours that blend so well – the different flower shapes also add greatly to the overall picture.*

INGREDIENTS

1 cascading geranium (*Pelargonium* 'Ville de Paris') **(A)**
1 purple petunia (*Petunia* 'Purple Wave') **(B)**
1 pink petunia (*Petunia* 'Bright Pink') **(C)**
2 blue lobelias (*Lobelia* 'Sapphire') **(D)**
1 pink begonia (*Begonia* × *tuberhybrida* 'Pink Cascade') **(E)**
2 yellow pansies (*Viola* 'Tutti Frutti') **(F)**
1 pink verbena (*Verbena* 'Sissinghurst') **(G)**
2 fuchsias (*Fuchsia* 'Mrs Popple') **(H)**
2 pink zonal geraniums (*Pelargonium* 'Emma Louise') **(I)**

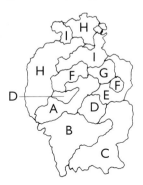

CONTAINER

40cm (16in) plastic-covered wire basket

MATERIALS

Liner
Lime-free (ericaceous) compost
Water-retaining granules
Slow-release fertilizer tablet or granules

POSITION

Hang in a sunny position to appreciate the rich colours.

PLANTING

1. Make up the basket in the spring and place it outside once the frosts have passed.

2. Hang or support the basket at a convenient height while you work, then add any liner that can be pierced.

3. Three-quarters fill the lined basket with the lime-free compost and add the water-retaining granules, together with the fertilizer granules, if you are using them. Mix well.

4. Make three holes in the front of the basket to take the purple and pink petunias and one of the lobelias. Plant these and continue to fill the basket with compost.

5. Plant a fuchsia at the back, along with its two attendant pink geraniums. In front of this group, plant the other fuchsia, the verbena, the trailing geranium and the begonia. Finally tuck in the two pansies and the remaining lobelia.

6. If you can manage to get your hand in, firm down the compost and push in the fertilizer tablet if used. Water.

MAINTENANCE

Water regularly. There is no need to feed if a slow-release fertilizer has been used. Deadhead when necessary.

Summer Freshness

*W*HITE OFTEN BRINGS *a touch of freshness to a basket, especially when it is seen against green or a dark background. In this basket the white is set off not only by the green foliage, but against the purple petunias, blue lobelias and the scarlet geraniums, which are all good foils. The white petunias are also echoed in the variegation of the leaves of the cornus. The shape works well, too, with the plants forming a round-bottomed cone, but as the season progresses, it will need regular care to maintain this shape.*

INGREDIENTS

1 young variegated cornus (*Cornus alba* 'Elegantissima') (**A**)
1 scarlet zonal geranium (*Pelargonium* 'Firebrand') (**B**)
3 white petunias (*Petunia* 'Falcon White') (**C**)
2 violet-blue petunias (*Petunia* 'Violet') (**D**)
1 scarlet ivy-leaved geranium (*Pelargonium* 'Decora Imperial') (**E**)
3 blue lobelias (*Lobelia* 'Sapphire') (**F**)

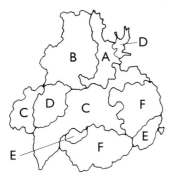

CONTAINER

35cm (14in) plastic-covered wire basket

MATERIALS

Liner
General-purpose compost
Water-retaining granules
Slow-release fertilizer tablet or granules

POSITION

Hang this display in a sunny or even a partly shaded site.

PLANTING

1. Plant up the basket in spring but keep it under cover until the frosts are finally over. It can be planted before it is hung outside, but will take longer to come into flower.

2. Hang the basket at a convenient working height or support it on a bucket or bowl to keep it stable. Place the liner in the basket and trim if necessary.

3. Three-quarters fill the basket with the compost and mix in the water-retaining granules. At the same time add the fertilizer granules if you are using them.

4. Cut three holes in the side of the liner and plant the three lobelias into them. Fill the rest of the basket with the compost and gently firm it down.

5. Add the other plants, starting with the zonal geranium and the variegated cornus. Next plant the four petunias, giving the white ones the most prominent positions. Finally, plant the ivy-leaved geranium, carefully training its wandering stems through the other plants.

6. Firm down the compost around the plants and level off the surface just below the rim of the basket. If you are using one, push a fertilizer tablet into the compost. Water well.

MAINTENANCE

Water regularly, especially in hot weather. If a slow-release fertilizer has been used there is no need for a liquid feed. Deadhead as necessary.

Pink Profusion

*P*INK IS A *popular colour for hanging baskets, and when it is used in profusion, as here, it is easy to see why. The pinks are soft enough not to be too overpowering but are a good contrast with the blue. Although you could use the plants listed below, there are plenty of alternative varieties of fuchsias and geraniums – as well as of the other plants – which would serve equally well in this display. This is a densely planted basket and care must be taken that it does not become too straggly.*

INGREDIENTS

1 pink ivy-leaved geranium (*Pelargonium* 'Amethyst') **(A)**
1 double fuchsia (*Fuchsia* 'Swingtime') **(B)**
2 diascias (*Diascia* 'Ruby Field') **(C)**
2 variegated ground ivies (*Glechoma hederacea* 'Variegata') **(D)**
1 violet verbena (*Verbena* 'Violet') **(E)**
2 blue lobelias (*Lobelia* 'Sapphire') **(F)**
1 purple zonal geranium (*Pelargonium* 'Karl Hagele') **(G)**

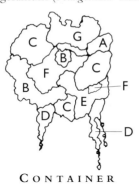

CONTAINER

35cm (14in) plastic-covered wire basket

MATERIALS

Liner
General-purpose compost
Water-retaining granules
Slow-release fertilizer tablet or granules

POSITION

This basket will grace any sunny wall.

PLANTING

1. These plants are frost tender and, although the basket can be prepared in advance, it should not be planted out until the threat of frost has passed.

2. To make it easier to prepare the basket, hang it at a working height. Alternatively, if the plants are not too far advanced, the basket can be placed in a bucket to hold it steady. Place the liner in the basket and, if necessary, trim.

3. Fill the basket three-quarters full with compost and add the water-retaining granules. At the same time you can also add the fertilizer granules if you are going to use them. Mix thoroughly.

4. Cut three holes in the liner and plant the ground ivies and one of the lobelias. Continue to fill the basket with compost and firm in lightly.

5. Plant up the rest of the basket, beginning with the geraniums towards the back. Next plant the fuchsia, followed by the diascias. Finally, put in the verbena and the other lobelia.

6. Carefully firm down the compost around the plants and level it off to about 2.5cm (1in) below the rim of the basket. If you are using one, add the fertilizer tablet at this stage. Water thoroughly.

MAINTENANCE

Water regularly. A liquid fertilizer will not be necessary.

Summer Mixture

THIS IS A colourful basket but one that can be simply created. Pansies are a welcome addition to arrangements of all kinds, and fuchsias are also a useful ingredient of many baskets, their curious shapes never failing to draw the eye. In this basket, a blowsy double fuchsia with purple underskirts dominates the scheme. The helichrysum is useful in pulling the whole display together, while the lobelia acts as a good background foil, although it has, unfortunately, been allowed to go past its best, leaving a blank area in the middle of the display.

INGREDIENTS

2 blue lobelias (*Lobelia* 'Sapphire') **(A)**
1 ivy-leaved geranium (*Pelargonium* 'Amethyst') **(B)**
3 mixed pansies (*Viola*) **(C)**
1 helichrysum (*Helichrysum petiolare*) **(D)**
1 yellow bidens (*Bidens* 'Golden Goddess') **(E)**
1 fuchsia (*Fuchsia* 'Blue Lake') **(F)**

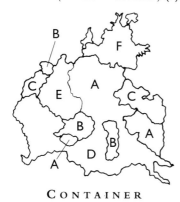

CONTAINER

30cm (12in) plastic-covered wire basket

MATERIALS

Liner
General-purpose compost
Water-retaining granules
Slow-release fertilizer tablet or granules

POSITION

Any sunny position will do for this basket.

PLANTING

1. Prepare the basket in the spring, but do not place it outside until the early summer, when the frosts should all be over.

2. Hang the basket at a convenient working height or place it in a bucket so that it is stable to work on. Line the basket and trim away any excess.

3. Add compost until the basket is about three-quarters full and mix in the water-retaining granules. If you are using fertilizer granules, add these at this point and mix the whole lot together. Fill up the rest of the basket with compost and firm it down lightly.

4. The fuchsia is the first plant to put in place. Set this towards the back of the basket and follow it with the three pansies. Next plant the bidens and then the helichrysum and the geranium. Finally, finish the basket with the lobelias.

5. Firm down the compost around the plants and add a fertilizer tablet if you have not used granules.

6. Thoroughly water with a watering can or by standing the basket in water.

MAINTENANCE

In spite of the water-retaining granules, the basket will require regular watering, but the slow-release fertilizer means there is no need for a liquid feed. Deadhead and remove any straggly stems that have finished flowering. If necessary, replace the lobelias with younger plants.

Purple and Gold

*P*URPLE PETUNIAS GIVE *a basket a wonderfully rich quality. The velvety trumpets glow with colour and lift the whole design. The deep colour of these petunias contrasts beautifully with the golden flowers of the bidens, which is an airy plant whose foliage and flowers are the perfect foil for the heavier petunias. Another delicate-looking plant, a blue lobelia, is tucked underneath. On the far side of the basket, pink geraniums also mix well with the petunias.*

INGREDIENTS

2 purple trailing petunias (*Petunia* 'Purple Wave') **(A)**
2 yellow bidens (*Bidens* 'Golden Goddess') **(B)**
2 pink ivy-leaved geraniums (*Pelargonium* 'Salmon Queen') **(C)**
1 blue lobelia (*Lobelia* 'Sapphire') **(D)**

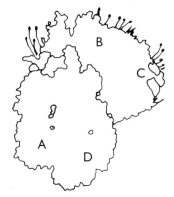

CONTAINER

30cm (12in) plastic-covered wire basket

MATERIALS

Liner
General-purpose compost
Water-retaining granules
Slow-release fertilizer tablet or granules

POSITION

Any sunny place will suit this display as long as
it is not too windy.

PLANTING

1. Make the basket up in the early summer, or plant it in spring and keep it under cover until the frosts have passed.

2. If possible hang the basket at a convenient working height or, if the plants are not too developed, support it on a bucket. Line the basket and trim off any that is not required.

3. Three-quarters fill the basket with a general-purpose compost and the water-retaining granules. Mix these in. Also mix in some fertilizer granules at this stage if you want to use them.

4. Make a slit in the liner and poke the lobelia through into the compost. Add more compost until the basket is full. Press it down slightly.

5. Plant the rest of the plants, starting with the petunias. Next put the two bidens in position and finally the two ivy-leaved geraniums.

6. Lightly firm the compost down around the plants and then smooth over the surface so that it is just below the rim of the basket. Add a fertilizer tablet if you have not used granules. Water thoroughly by standing the basket in water or by using a watering can.

MAINTENANCE

Water regularly, but there is no need to feed if you used a slow-release fertilizer. Cut back wayward stems and remove dead flowers.

Butterflies

A HANGING BASKET filled with a single type of plant can look boring, but sometimes it can create a wonderful effect, as in this basket filled with one type of regal geranium, although it must be said that it would look better against a plain, uncluttered background. The bicoloured flowers stand out well against the tight ball of dark green foliage, looking just like a cloud of hovering butterflies. The two-tone flowers break up what would, had a single colour been used, be a dull arrangement and give it liveliness and interest.

INGREDIENTS

7 regal geraniums (*Pelargonium* 'Captain Starlight') **(A)**

CONTAINER

30cm (12in) plastic-covered wire basket

MATERIALS

Liner
General-purpose compost
Water-retaining granules
Slow-release fertilizer tablet or granules

POSITION

This basket can hang in a sunny position or in one that is out of the sun for part of the day. The flowers would stand out against a dark background.

PLANTING

1. All pelargoniums are tender and must not be put outside until after the frosts have finished. To get it off to a good start, however, plant the basket in spring and hang it in a conservatory or greenhouse until it is safe to move it outside.

2. If the plants do not get in the way, stand the basket on a bucket to work on it; otherwise, hang at a convenient working height. Line the basket.

3. Three-quarters fill the basket with a general-purpose compost and add the water-retaining granules. Mix well. Also add fertilizer granules at this stage if you wish.

4. Make three slits in the liner and plant three of the geraniums in the front lower half of the basket. Fill the remainder of the basket and firm down gently. Plant the remaining four geraniums.

5. Firm down the compost around the plants and level off the surface to about 2.5cm (1in) below the rim of the basket. Add the fertilizer tablet if you are using one.

6. Water thoroughly by standing the basket in a bucket of water or watering carefully with a watering can.

MAINTENANCE

Little maintenance is required and there is no need to feed. Watering should be regular to ensure that the compost does not dry out. Deadhead if necessary.

Peeping Lizzie

*T*HE AIRY STEMS *and flowers of the lobelias create a haze through which the busy lizzies peep. Also peeping through the cloud of lobelias are the pale, immature leaves of the lamium, which will, later in the summer, produce flowers that will be at odds with the design and should be removed. This is a basket for special occasions, for it is unlikely to last in its pristine condition for too long because the lobelias will become congested and lax and the busy lizzies will grow too large. Enjoy it while it is at its best.*

INGREDIENTS

4 pink busy lizzies (*Impatiens*) (A)
1 white busy lizzie (*Impatiens*) (B)
1 variegated lamium (*Lamium maculatum*) (C)
6 blue lobelias (*Lobelia* 'Sapphire') (D)

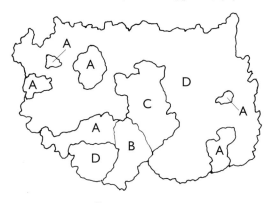

CONTAINER

30cm (12in) plastic-covered wire basket

MATERIALS

Liner
General-purpose compost
Water-retaining granules
Slow-release fertilizer tablet or granules

POSITION

A sunny position or one in light shade will be suitable
for this basket.

PLANTING

1. Although the lamium is hardy, the other plants are tender and should not be exposed to the frost. Make up the basket but keep it under cover in a conservatory or greenhouse until it is safe to put it outdoors.

2. Hang the basket at a convenient height or support it in a suitable bucket while you work. Put in the liner and trim off any excess.

3. Three-quarters fill the basket with compost. Add the water-retaining granules and some fertilizer granules if you are using them. Mix them together.

4. Cut holes in the liner and poke in the busy lizzies, with the white one in the front. Fill the rest of the basket with more compost and lightly press it down.

5. Plant the surface of the basket, starting with the lamium. Surround this with the six lobelias.

6. Carefully press the compost down around each of the plants, and, if you are using one, push a fertilizer tablet into the compost.

7. Water thoroughly by standing it in a bucket of water or with a watering can.

MAINTENANCE

Water once a day. If you have not used a slow-release fertilizer, the basket will need a liquid feed once a week.

Orange and Red

*T*HIS IS A *simple basket, but one that is effective for all that. It consists of only three types of plants, and yet it looks full of life and colour. The orange of the nasturtiums and the scarlet of the geraniums go well together, both being shown off well against their respective foliage. Both are trailing plants, but the real waterfall is created by the variegated ground ivies. Bright colours such as these need to be carefully positioned – this blue door is perfect.*

INGREDIENTS

2 red ivy-leaved geraniums (*Pelargonium* 'Lily Marlene') **(A)**
2 variegated ground ivies (*Glechoma hederacea* 'Variegata') **(B)**
2 nasturtiums (*Tropaeolum majus*) **(C)**

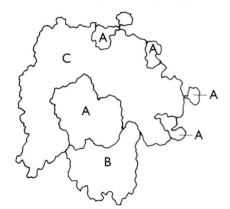

CONTAINER

40cm (16in) plastic-covered wire basket

MATERIALS

Liner
General-purpose compost
Water-retaining granules
Slow-release fertilizer tablet or granules

POSITION

Hang the basket in sunny place or one that receives sun for at least part of the day.

PLANTING

1. Plant this basket up when the plants become available, but wait until the last frosts have passed before putting it outside.

2. Hang the basket at a convenient height while you work. Line it and trim off any liner that protrudes above the rim.

3. Pour a general-purpose compost into the basket until it is about three-quarters full, then add the water-retaining granules. Mix in the fertilizer granules if you are using them.

4. Make two slits in the liner and plant the ground ivies through the holes. Continue to fill the basket with compost until it is full. Lightly press this down.

5. Now plant the top surface of the basket, starting with the geraniums. Then add the nasturtiums. If they are already big enough to trail, arrange the stems over the side of the basket.

6. Gently firm down the compost around the plants and level off the surface so that it is about 2.5cm (1in) below the rim of the basket. Insert the fertilizer tablet if used.

7. Water thoroughly, either by standing the basket in water or by watering it from above with a watering can.

MAINTENANCE

The compost should not be allowed to dry out, but neither should it be kept wringing wet. If you use a slow-release fertilizer, there is no need for further feeding. Remove dead heads and stray stems to keep the display tidy.

Silver Lining

*I*T WOULD SEEM *that most gardeners feel that hanging baskets should always be made up of brightly coloured plants. This is far from the truth, however, and many beautiful baskets can be designed using pale colours. They need careful siting, however, or they will be lost or overpowered by their surroundings. This tranquil mixture of grey and pink is created by the foliage of the helichrysums, which provides a restful setting for the flowers of the geraniums, whose pale green leaves complement those of the helichrysums.*

INGREDIENTS

2 helichrysums (*Helichrysum petiolare*) **(A)**
3 pink ivy-leaved geraniums (*Pelargonium* 'La France') **(B)**

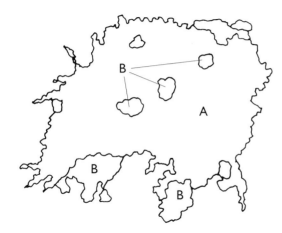

CONTAINER

30cm (12in) plastic-covered wire basket

MATERIALS

Liner
General-purpose compost
Water-retaining granules
Slow-release fertilizer tablet or granules

POSITION

An open, sunny position is best.

PLANTING

1. Do not prepare this basket until after the last frosts have passed. It is possible to create it earlier but if you do, keep it protected in a conservatory or greenhouse and do not bring it out until early summer.

2. Hang the basket at a convenient height for working. Insert a liner of your choice and trim off any that sticks up above the rim.

3. Three-quarters fill the basket with a general-purpose compost and mix in the water-retaining granules. If you are using fertilizer granules, now is the time to mix them in, too. Continue to fill the basket with compost until it reaches the rim and then pack it down lightly.

4. The planting is very simple. First plant the geraniums and then the helichrysums. Carefully arrange any stems that are already trailing over the edge of the basket and avoid breaking them.

5. Gently firm the compost around the roots of the plants and level off the surface at about 2.5cm (1in) below the rim of the basket. If you are using a fertilizer tablet, push it into the soil at this point. Water thoroughly.

MAINTENANCE

This should not need as much watering as some other baskets, but even so the soil should not be allowed to dry out. There is no need to feed.

Bright Days

*B*RIGHTLY COLOURED BASKETS *lift the spirits, and it is difficult to feel anything but pleasure when one looks at a design full of glowing colours. This brilliantly coloured basket does not shrink into the background but comes straight out and welcomes you. The dominant colours are the reds and bright pinks of the geraniums and busy lizzies, which are always good basket plants – colourful and long lasting, yet easy to obtain.*

INGREDIENTS

2 red petunias (*Petunia* 'Falcon Red') (A)
2 scarlet ivy-leaved geraniums (*Pelargonium* 'Lily Marlene') (B)
2 blue felicias (*Felicia amelloides*) (C)
4 mixed busy lizzies (*Impatiens*) (D)
2 mini cascade geraniums (*Pelargonium* 'Red Mini Cascade') (E)
2 purple verbenas (*Verbena* 'Violet') (F)
2 blue lobelias (*Lobelia* 'Sapphire') (G)

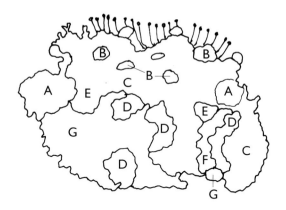

CONTAINER

35cm (14in) plastic-covered wire basket

MATERIALS

Liner
General-purpose compost
Water-retaining granules
Slow-release fertilizer tablet or granules

POSITION

A sunny wall is best, although the display will take a little shade for part of the day.

PLANTING

1. Prepare the basket in spring, but keep it under glass until the last frosts have passed.

2. To make it easier to work with, hang the basket at a convenient height or support it in a bucket. Put in a liner and trim it level with the rim if necessary.

3. Three-quarters fill the basket with a general-purpose compost. Mix into this water-retaining granules and, if you wish, fertilizer granules.

4. Cut six holes around the front half of the basket and plant the lobelias, two busy lizzies and the verbenas through into the compost. Fill the basket with compost and firm down.

5. Add the ivy-leaved geraniums, then the felicias and petunias. Work your way forwards with the cascade geraniums and, finally, the other busy lizzies.

6. Level off the compost, firming it down around the plants. The final surface should be just below the rim of the basket. Bury the fertilizer tablet if used. Water thoroughly.

MAINTENANCE

Water the basket once a day and deadhead as necessary.

Gold and Blue

*Y*ELLOW AND BLUE *are always a good combination in the garden, the two colours not only complement-*
ing each other beautifully, but also usually creating a wonderfully fresh look. There are any number of
different plants that will give this effect, but for hanging baskets one of the best combinations is a yellow
bidens mixed with the dark blue of a lobelia. A bright red verbena has been added to this arrangement for a
bit more drama, but it has all but retired into the shadows. The helichrysum at the top lightens the effect.

INGREDIENTS

2 yellow bidens (*Bidens* 'Golden Goddess') **(A)**
2 blue lobelia (*Lobelia* 'Sapphire') **(B)**
1 scarlet verbena (*Verbena peruviana*) **(C)**
1 helichrysum (*Helichrysum petiolare*) **(D)**

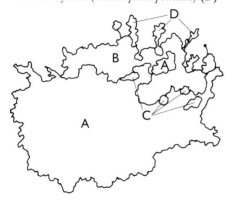

CONTAINER

35cm (14in) plastic-covered wire basket

MATERIALS

Liner
General-purpose compost
Water-retaining granules
Slow-release fertilizer tablet or granules

POSITION

This basket should be hung in a light, sunny position or it
will become leggy and begin to look untidy.

PLANTING

1. This display should not be put out in the open until the
   threat of frost has passed. It can be prepared earlier but
   should be kept under cover until early summer.

2. Hang the basket at a convenient height or stand it in a
   bucket while you work. Cut the liner to fit the basket and
   put it in position.

3. Pour the compost into the basket until it is about three-
   quarters full. Add the water-retaining granules and mix
   them in, and mix in the fertilizer granules if
   you are using them. Finish filling the
   basket with compost, level off the
   surface and press it down lightly.

4. Start by planting the helichrysum at
   the back of the basket. Next position
   the verbena on the right. Follow this
   with the lobelias and finally add the
   bidens.

5. Carefully manoeuvre between the stems and gently firm
   down the compost, pressing it down around the plants.
   Level off the surface so that it is about 2.5cm (1in) below
   the rim. If used, push a fertilizer tablet into the compost.
   Water thoroughly.

MAINTENANCE

Water regularly, keeping the compost moist. There is no need
to feed if a slow-release fertilizer has been used. Deadhead
regularly and trim off any straggly stems.

Simplicity

*T*HIS IS A *delightful combination of plants, which is simple to achieve and yet is very effective. The simplicity is helped by the fact that the flowers have remained in distinct groups rather than mingling together. It is also helped by the colour combination. The bright begonias immediately attract the eye, which then tends to wander off to the sugary pink busy lizzie. This colour is then reflected in the geranium below. The fuchsias create a thread that runs through the scheme and finally tails off with the ground ivy.*

INGREDIENTS

1 orange-red begonia (*Begonia* × *tuberhybrida* 'Crimson Cascade') **(A)**
1 pink busy lizzie (*Impatiens*) **(B)**
1 pink fuchsia (*Fuchsia* 'Jack Acland') **(C)**
2 pink ivy-leaved geraniums (*Pelargonium* 'Bridesmaid') **(D)**
1 variegated ground ivy (*Glechoma hederacea* 'Variegata') **(E)**
2 blue lobelias (*Lobelia* 'Sapphire') **(F)**
1 pink and red fuchsia (*Fuchsia* 'Orange Mirage') **(G)**

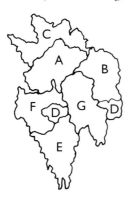

CONTAINER

30cm (12in) plastic-covered wire basket

MATERIALS

Liner
Lime-free (ericaceous) compost
Water-retaining granules
Slow-release fertilizer tablet or granules

POSITION

This basket will prefer a partly shaded position, especially during the hottest part of the day. Avoid a windy site.

PLANTING

1. Prepare the basket in spring but do not place it outside until after the last frosts have gone.

2. Hang the basket at a convenient height or stand it on a bucket. Fit a liner into the basket,.

3. Begonias do not like lime, so use a lime-free compost. Three-quarters fill the basket, then mix in the water-retaining granules and, if you wish, the fertilizer granules.

4. Make two slits towards the top of the liner and push the lobelias through into the compost. Make another slit lower down and insert the ground ivy.

5. Continue filling the basket until the compost reaches the rim. Add the pink fuchsia. The begonia should be next, followed by the busy lizzie, the geraniums and, finally, the other fuchsia.

6. Firm down the compost and level off just below the rim. Add a fertilizer tablet if you are using one. Water.

MAINTENANCE

Water this basket regularly and deadhead when necessary.

High Summer

*H*ERE WE HAVE *a basket that is crammed full of summer flowers. As you came out of the house, you could be in no doubt about the time of year, whatever the weather. The pinks and blues, which are so evocative of high summer, are attractively combined in this arrangement, while the yellow of the bidens at the sides of the basket contrasts with the more sombre colours. Many of the flowers are borne on long stems, which give the whole display a floating look.*

INGREDIENTS

1 pink verbena (*Verbena* 'Sissinghurst') **(A)**
3 pink petunias (*Petunia* 'Pink Perfection') **(B)**
2 ivy-leaved geraniums (*Pelargonium* 'Red Mini Cascade') **(C)**
1 fuchsia (*Fuchsia* 'Indian Maid') **(D)**
2 yellow bidens (*Bidens* 'Golden Goddess') **(E)**
1 Swan River daisy (*Brachycome iberidifolia* 'Blue Star') **(F)**
1 variegated ground ivy (*Glechoma hederacea* 'Variegata') **(G)**
1 helichrysum (*Helichrysum petiolare*) **(H)**
1 blue lobelia (*Lobelia* 'Sapphire') **(I)**
1 white lobelia (*Lobelia* 'White Cascade') **(J)**

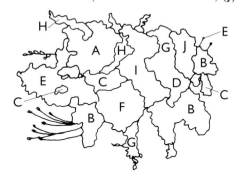

CONTAINER

30cm (12in) plastic-covered wire basket

MATERIALS

Liner
General-purpose compost
Water-retaining granules
Slow-release fertilizer tablet or granules

POSITION

Ideally, this basket should hang against a sunny wall.

PLANTING

1. The planting can be carried out in spring, but do not put out the basket until early summer, when the frosts have passed.

2. Hang the basket at a convenient working height or stand it in a bucket. Line the basket with your preferred lining.

3. Fill the basket about three-quarters full with a general-purpose compost, and mix into this the water-retaining granules. If you are using them, also add fertilizer granules.

4. Cut four holes in the liner and plant the two bidens, the Swan River daisy and the variegated ground ivy.

5. Fill the remainder of the basket with compost, then start planting at the back with the helichrysum. Follow this with the verbena to the side and the two geraniums slightly in front. Next come the fuchsia and the petunias. Last, tuck in the two lobelias.

6. Firm down the compost around the plants and level off the surface just below the rim of the basket. Push the fertilizer tablet down into the compost if you are using one. Water.

MAINTENANCE

Water every day. There is no need to feed if slow-release fertilizers have been used. Remove any dead flowers.

Fuchsia Cascade

*S*OME GARDENERS BECOME *fanatical about one type of plant and tend to grow them to the exclusion of anything else. Fuchsias, for example, seem to get into some people's blood, and they become collectors and real experts at growing them. The advantage of fuchsias is that although most are grown as bushes, some can be grown as 'standards', like miniature trees, and there are some that trail and are absolutely perfect for hanging baskets. You do not need to be an expert to grow or appreciate this basket of four kinds of fuchsia.*

INGREDIENTS

1 Swingtime fuchsia (*Fuchsia* 'Swingtime') **(A)**
1 Blue Satin fuchsia (*Fuchsia* 'Blue Satin') **(B)**
1 Cascade fuchsia (*Fuchsia* 'Cascade') **(C)**
1 Lilac Time fuchsia (*Fuchsia* 'Lilac Time') **(D)**

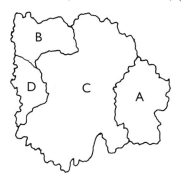

CONTAINER

40cm (16in) plastic-covered wire basket

MATERIALS

Liner
General-purpose compost
Water-retaining granules
Slow-release fertilizer tablet or granules

POSITION

Fuchsias prefer to be placed where they do not receive the full heat of the midday sun, but they should not be in too much shade.

PLANTING

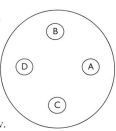

1. While some fuchsias are hardy, many are not, so do not be in too much of a hurry to put the basket outside. Wait until the frosts have passed.

2. Hang the basket at a convenient height to make it easier to work on, then line the basket and trim off any excess liner.

3. Part fill the basket with a general-purpose compost. Add some water-retaining granules and mix in. If you want to use fertilizer granules, these should also be added now.

4. Finish filling the basket to the brim with compost, then plant the fuchsias, spacing them evenly across the surface of the compost and planting them to about the same depth as they were in their original pots.

5. Firm down the compost around each fuchsia and level off the surface so that it is about 2.5cm (1in) below the rim of the basket. If you want to use a fertilizer tablet instead of the granules, push it down into the soil at this stage.

6. Water thoroughly by standing in a bucket of water or from above with a watering can.

MAINTENANCE

The water-retaining granules will help the plants through the hottest days but they will still need regular watering. If slow-release fertilizer has been used there is no need to feed. Deadhead as necessary.

Fancy Edges

Picotee flowers — those whose petals are edged in a different colour — are a valuable asset to the owner of hanging baskets. They produce such a startling, busy effect that anyone glancing at the display would think that twice the number of flowers had been used. The power of this arrangement is further enhanced by the hundreds of tiny lobelia flowers. The more solid tones of the red petunias and yellow calceolaria calm the effect slightly, but this is still an arrangement that is bursting with energy.

INGREDIENTS

2 picotee ivy-leaved geraniums (*Pelargonium* 'Rouletta') **(A)**
1 red petunia (*Petunia* 'Falcon Red') **(B)**
1 purple picotee petunia (*Petunia* 'Purple Picotee') **(C)**
1 yellow calceolaria (*Calceolaria* 'Sunshine') **(D)**
3 pink lobelias (*Lobelia* 'Lilac Cascade') **(E)**
1 rich red petunia (*Petunia* 'Velvet Mirage') **(F)**

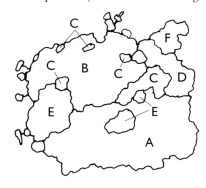

CONTAINER

30cm (12in) plastic-covered wire basket

MATERIALS

Liner
General-purpose compost
Water-retaining granules
Slow-release fertilizer tablet or granules

POSITION

A sunny wall protected from the worst of the wind will be ideal.

PLANTING

1. Spring is the best time to plant up this basket, but do not put it outside until the last of the frosts has passed because all the plants are tender.

2. Support the basket on a bucket or large flowerpot or hang it at a convenient height while you work. Place the liner in the basket and trim it to size if necessary.

3. Part fill the basket with a general-purpose compost and mix in the water-retaining granules. If you are using them, also mix in some fertilizer granules.

4. Cut three holes in the liner and plant the lobelias through them.

5. Continue to add compost until the basket is full, packing it down slightly around the roots of the lobelia. Then add the two plain petunias, followed by the picotee petunia. Next tuck in the calceolaria and finally the two picotee geraniums in the front of the basket.

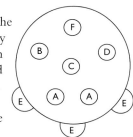

6. Gently firm down the compost around the plants and level off the surface so that it comes just below the rim of the basket. If you are using a fertilizer tablet, now is the time to push it into the compost. Water thoroughly.

MAINTENANCE

Water this display regularly and deadhead when necessary.

Red Cascade

THIS BASKET HAS a Continental flavour, and it is the type of display you might expect to see in France. It is a ball of small-petalled geraniums, all the same bright red and beautifully set off against the shiny green foliage. The simplicity is stunning: just four plants and you have a result that is worth a gold medal in any hanging basket competition. It looks best set against a foliage background as here, and although soft-coloured brick or stone would be perfectly sympathetic, some types of wall might be wholly inappropriate.

INGREDIENTS

4 red cascade geraniums (*Pelargonium* 'Mini Red Cascade') **(A)**

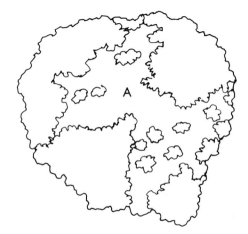

CONTAINER

30cm (12in) plastic-covered wire basket

MATERIALS

Liner
General-purpose compost
Water-retaining granules
Slow-release fertilizer tablet or granules

POSITION

A sunny or lightly shaded position will suit the plants in this basket.

PLANTING

1. Although geraniums will stand a degree or two of frost without too much damage, it is best not to hang out this basket until after the frosts have passed. It can, however, be prepared in advance so that the plants are in bloom when it is finally put out.

2. Stand the basket on a bucket or hang it at a convenient height so that it is easy to work at. Insert the liner of your choice, trimming the edges back as necessary.

3. Three-quarters fill the basket with a general-purpose compost and mix into it the water-retaining granules. If you decide to use fertilizer granules rather than a tablet, now is the time to add them. Mix them well with the compost.

4. Continue to fill the basket with compost and press it down lightly. Plant the four geraniums in a regular pattern. Press down the compost between the plants and level off the surface so that the final level is about 2.5cm (1in) below the rim of the basket. Insert the fertilizer tablet at this stage if you are using one.

5. Water thoroughly, either by standing the basket in a bowl of water or from above by using a watering can.

MAINTENANCE

Very little maintenance is required except regular watering. If slow-release fertilizers have been used there is no need to use a liquid feed. Remove trusses of dead flowers.

Monkey Business

THIS IS AN unusual basket but one that will give a great deal of pleasure. The geraniums and busy lizzies are reasonably standard fare, but the use of mimulus, or monkey flowers, with their cheeky faces, is a lovely touch. The yellow of the mimulus brightens the basket, while the deep pinks and reds of the geranium and busy lizzies add a richness to the overall picture. As long as the mimulus is not allowed to dry out or become too straggly, this display should last for a long time.

INGREDIENTS

1 scented-leaved geranium (*Pelargonium* 'Clorinda') **(A)**
2 deep pink busy lizzies (*Impatiens*) **(B)**
1 mimulus (*Mimulus* 'Viva') **(C)**
1 red busy lizzie (*Impatiens*) **(D)**

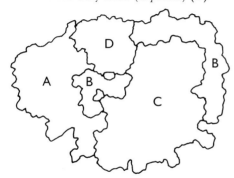

CONTAINER

30cm (12in) plastic-covered wire basket

MATERIALS

Liner
General-purpose compost
Water-retaining granules
Slow-release fertilizer tablet or granules

POSITION

This basket hangs in an alcove, but it could be hung on any wall, although preferably one that misses the sun during the hottest part of the day.

PLANTING

1. The basket should not be assembled outside before the early summer, although it can be put together earlier if it is kept under cover.

2. Support the basket on a bucket or hang it at a convenient height while you work. Fit a liner into the basket and trim it to shape if necessary.

3. Three-quarters fill the basket with a general-purpose compost. Mix into this the water-retaining granules and some fertilizer granules if you are using them.

4. Fill the remainder of the basket with compost and lightly firm it down.

5. Start by putting in the geranium followed by the two pink busy lizzies. Next plant the red busy lizzie and finally the mimulus, taking care not to break any of the stems of the mimulus, which can be brittle.

6. Gently firm down the compost around the plants and level it off so that the surface is about 2.5cm (1in) below the rim of the basket. Add a fertilizer tablet if you want to use one.

7. Thoroughly water from below by standing the basket in a bowl of water or from above with a watering can.

MAINTENANCE

It is important to water regularly so that neither the impatiens nor the mimulus dries out. Deadhead as often as necessary.

Mixed Bag

THIS HANGING BASKET contains a mixed bag of plants, some trailing and some erect, which gives the impression that it is a very tall display rather than the more usual rounded shape. The principal colours are reds and pinks, with the white of the bacopas and petunias creating flashes of light among the dark green foliage. There is plenty of foliage in this display, and it might seem to swamp the flowers, a problem that could be avoided by using another red geranium and only one nasturtium.

INGREDIENTS

1 pink zonal geranium (*Pelargonium* 'Gold Fringe') (**A**)
1 red cascade geranium (*Pelargonium* 'Red Mini Cascade') (**B**)
3 white bacopas (*Sutera cordata* 'Snowflake') (**C**)
2 red nasturtiums (*Tropaeolum majus*) (**D**)
1 trailing petunia (*Petunia* 'Blue Vein') (**E**)
2 blue lobelias (*Lobelia* 'Sapphire') (**F**)

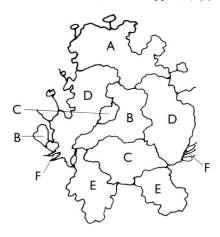

CONTAINER

30cm (12in) plastic-covered wire basket

MATERIALS

Liner
General-purpose compost
Water-retaining granules
Slow-release fertilizer tablet or granules

POSITION

Any sunny wall will do, but avoid a windy site.

PLANTING

1. It is best to make up this basket in advance and keep it under glass, until early summer begins.

2. Because of its trailing nature it will be easier to work on this basket if it is hung at a convenient height. Line the basket and trim off any excess that protrudes above the rim.

3. Part fill the basket with a general-purpose compost and add the water-retaining granules. If you want to use fertilizer granules, mix them in now.

4. Cut three holes in the liner and plant the two lobelias and one of the bacopas. Top up the basket with compost, firming it down around the roots of the three plants.

5. Plant the rest of the basket, starting with the zonal geranium at the back. Then plant the cascade geranium, followed by the two nasturtiums. Finally, plant the petunia and tuck in the remaining two bacopas on either side.

6. Firm down the compost gently and level off the surface just below the rim of the basket. Push in a fertilizer tablet if you are using one and water thoroughly.

MAINTENANCE

Water regularly and remove any fading flowers.

Pink Ball

SIMPLICITY IS OFTEN the keynote to a good basket. Here, the number of different plants has been restricted, as has the number of colours, and the different pinks work well together, especially against the green foliage. Pinching out any wayward stems will help prevent the display from becoming too wild-looking and it should flower over a long period. Both fuchsias and busy lizzies are happy in light shade, so this is a versatile basket, which can be used in a range of situations.

INGREDIENTS

1 bush fuchsia (*Fuchsia* 'Santa Cruz') **(A)**
1 red petunia (*Petunia* 'Falcon Red') **(B)**
2 pink busy lizzies (*Impatiens*) **(C)**
1 trailing fuchsia (*Fuchsia* 'Jack Acland') **(D)**
2 blue lobelias (*Lobelia* 'Sapphire') **(E)**

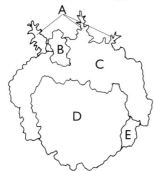

CONTAINER

30cm (12in) plastic-covered wire basket

MATERIALS

Liner
General-purpose compost
Water-retaining granules
Slow-release fertilizer tablet or granules

POSITION

Hang in light shade or sun, although preferably not where it will be in full sun during the hottest part of the day.

PLANTING

1. Plant up the basket in mid-spring but do not put it outdoors until the threat of frosts has passed because some of these plants are tender.

2. Stand the basket on a bucket or large flowerpot or hang it at a convenient height while you work. Line the basket with your preferred liner, trimming off the excess if necessary.

3. Part fill the basket with a general-purpose compost and mix into it the water-retaining granules. At this stage you can also mix in fertilizer granules if you wish.

4. Cut two holes in the liner and insert a lobelia through each. Fill up the rest of the basket, gently firming the compost around the roots of the lobelias.

5. Plant the basket, starting with the bush fuchsia at the back. In front of this and to one side, position the petunia and then add the two busy lizzies. Finally, place the trailing fuchsia at the front and fan out its stems over the edge.

6. Gently firm down the compost around the plants and level off the surface so that it is about 2.5cm (1in) below the rim of the basket. Push a fertilizer tablet into the soil if you are using one. Water thoroughly.

MAINTENANCE

Water this basket regularly and deadhead as necessary.

Profusion

COTTAGE GARDENS ARE renowned for their profusion of flowers, and this basket is very reminiscent of this kind of garden. It is so packed with plants that the flowers seem to be bursting out in all directions. Shades of pink dominate, although the golden-yellow of the bidens shines out and catches the eye. The waves of lobelia combine with the different foliages to create the background colour. This basket will need some looking after to make certain that it does not become too straggly and lose its effect.

INGREDIENTS

1 red petunia (*Petunia* 'Falcon Red') **(A)**
2 yellow bidens (*Bidens* 'Golden Goddess') **(B)**
1 helichrysum (*Helichrysum petiolare*) **(C)**
1 pink ivy-leaved geranium (*Pelargonium* 'La France') **(D)**
1 cascade geranium (*Pelargonium* 'Rose Mini Cascade') **(E)**
1 trailing fuchsia (*Fuchsia* 'Orange Mirage') **(F)**
2 lilac lobelias (*Lobelia* 'Lilac Cascade') **(G)**
1 purple verbena (*Verbena* 'Purple Delight') **(H)**

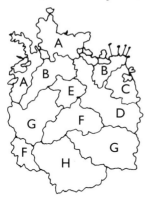

CONTAINER

40cm (16in) plastic-covered wire basket

MATERIALS

Liner
General-purpose compost
Water-retaining granules
Slow-release fertilizer tablet or granules

POSITION

The ideal position for this hanging basket would be a sunny wall that is protected from strong or gusty winds.

PLANTING

1. Prepare the basket in spring, but keep it under glass until the last of the frosts have passed because all the plants are tender.

2. Hang the basket at a convenient height or support it on a bucket or flowerpot while you work. Insert a liner and trim off any excess protruding above the rim of the basket.

3. Three-quarters fill the basket with a general-purpose compost. Mix into this the water-retaining granules and, if you want to use them, a quantity of fertilizer granules.

4. Cut a hole in the centre of the front half of the basket and plant the verbena through into the compost.

5. Continue to fill the basket with compost and firm it down around the roots of the verbena. Plant the rest of the plants, starting with the petunia towards the back. Work forwards, finishing off with the two lobelias.

6. Level off the compost, firming it down around the plants. The final surface should be just below the rim of the basket. Bury the fertilizer tablet if you are using one. Water well.

MAINTENANCE

Water the basket regularly and deadhead the flowers as necessary.

Subtle Shades

COOL COLOURS ARE always welcome during a hot summer, and this arrangement looks especially delightful against the white door and the soft colour of the old stone. White and other pale colours contrast well with foliage, and here the flowers are set off not only by the leaves within the basket but also those of the shrub on the wall behind. The most eye-catching plant in this design is the begonia with its flamboyant blooms, and their white is picked up in the petunia and the busy lizzie. Colour is provided by the daisies and lobelias.

INGREDIENTS

1 white begonia (*Begonia × tuberhybrida* 'Bridal Cascade') (**A**)
2 yellow daisies (*Argyranthemum* 'Jamaica Primrose') (**B**)
1 plectranthus (*Plectranthus coleoides* 'Variegatus') (**C**)
1 white busy lizzie (*Impatiens*) (**D**)
2 blue lobelias (*Lobelia* 'Light Blue Basket') (**E**)
1 lime green helichrysum (*Helichrysum petiolare* 'Limelight') (**F**)
1 white petunia (*Petunia* 'White') (**G**)

CONTAINER

30cm (12in) plastic-covered wire basket

MATERIALS

Liner
Lime-free (ericaceous) compost
Water-retaining granules
Slow-release fertilizer tablet or granules

POSITION

The begonia would appreciate a sunny position but one that is not in the hot midday sun.

PLANTING

1. Make up the basket in early summer, once the frosts have passed. Alternatively, prepare it in spring and keep it hanging in a conservatory or greenhouse until it can be safely put outdoors.

2. Although it is often easier to work with the basket held in a bucket, if plants are already trailing, it is best to hang it at a convenient working height. Line the basket, trimming the liner to size as necessary.

3. Three-quarters fill the basket with a lime-free compost. Mix into this the water-retaining granules. If you are using fertilizer granules, now is the time to add these as well.

4. Cut two slits in the liner and poke through the roots of the two lobelias. Continue to add compost, firming it down gently around the roots of the lobelias.

5. Next, plant the begonia and follow this with the helichrysum in the centre. Then add the petunia and busy lizzie, followed by the plectranthus and finally the two daisies.

6. Firm down the compost gently, finishing it off about 2.5cm (1in) below the rim of the basket. Press a fertilizer tablet into the compost if you have not used granules. Water thoroughly.

MAINTENANCE

Water the basket regularly and deadhead the flowers as necessary.

Summer Sunshine

*S*TRONG COLOURS SET *against the soft colour of the stone wall are the keynote to this display, which glows in the summer sun. The brightness of the reds and yellows is perfectly contrasted with the softer foliage of the helichrysum and with the dainty filigree of the bidens leaves. Softer colours, from the petunias and the lobelia, have been added to cool the picture slightly, although the lobelia is still partially hidden deep in the foliage. The plants will need to be cut back occasionally if the arrangement is not to become too wild.*

INGREDIENTS

1 scarlet zonal geranium (*Pelargonium* 'Paul Crampel') **(A)**
2 red cascade ivy-leaved geraniums (*Pelargonium* 'Mini Red Cascade') **(B)**
2 yellow bidens (*Bidens* 'Golden Goddess') **(C)**
2 petunias (*Petunia* 'Carpet Mixed') **(D)**
1 helichrysum (*Helichrysum petiolare*) **(E)**
1 lilac lobelia (*Lobelia* 'Lilac Cascade') **(F)**

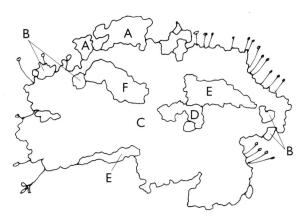

CONTAINER

40cm (16in) plastic-covered wire basket

MATERIALS

Liner
General-purpose compost
Water-retaining granules
Slow-release fertilizer tablet or granules

POSITION

A sunny site is best for this basket; avoid a windy position.

PLANTING

1. Do not prepare this basket until after the last frosts have passed. If you do plant it earlier, keep it in a conservatory or greenhouse and do not bring it out until early summer.

2. Hang the basket at a convenient height, or, if the plants are not too trailing, support it on a bucket while you work. Line the basket with the liner of your choice, trimming it to fit if necessary.

3. Three-quarters fill the basket with a general-purpose compost and mix in the water-retaining granules. If you are using fertilizer granules, now is the time to mix them in too. Continue to fill the basket with compost and tamp it down lightly.

4. Plant the red geranium at the back of the basket first. Next, position the other two geraniums on either side, with the helichrysum in the centre, between them. Finally, add the other plants around the front of the basket.

5. Gently firm the compost around the roots of the plants and level off the surface to just below the rim of the basket. If you are using a fertilizer tablet, push it into the soil at this point. Water thoroughly.

MAINTENANCE

This hanging basket will need to be watered regularly.

All Change

*T*HIS HALF-BASKET, *which is attached directly to a wall, is packed full of colourful plants. The main feature of the display is the pink geraniums, which create a sugary topping to the mixture of colours. At the moment they are the perfect accompaniment for the dark blue lobelias, but later in the season they are likely to be overtaken by the bright yellows of the mimulus, French marigolds and calceolaria. Changing the colour scheme of a basket as the season progresses by careful plant selection can give you two baskets for the price of one.*

INGREDIENTS

3 pink zonal geraniums (*Pelargonium* 'Highfield Pink') **(A)**
2 yellow French marigolds (*Tagetes* 'Calico Yellow') **(B)**
2 mimulus (*Mimulus* 'Calypso Mixed') **(C)**
1 calceolaria (*Calceolaria* 'Sunshine') **(D)**
3 blue lobelias (*Lobelia* 'Sapphire') **(E)**
1 helichrysum (*Helichrysum petiolare*) **(F)**
2 trailing fuchsias (*Fuchsia* 'Orange Mirage') **(G)**

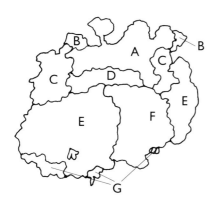

CONTAINER

60cm (24in) half-basket

MATERIALS

Liner
General-purpose compost
Water-retaining granules
Slow-release fertilizer tablet or granules

POSITION

Any sunny wall will be a suitable site for this basket.

PLANTING

1. If this basket is fitted permanently to a wall, make it up after frosts are over. If it can be taken down, make it up in spring and keep it under glass until early summer.

2. These baskets are not easy to fill if they are not either hanging on a wall or propped up in some way. If you want to prevent water dripping down the wall, you will need a waterproof liner, but this will prevent you from inserting plants in the sides of the basket.

3. Half fill the basket with compost and add the water-retaining granules and, if you wish, fertilizer granules. Mix them together.

4. Cut holes in the liner and plant the lobelias, helichrysum and fuchsias. Continue to add compost, firming it down around the plants. Plant up the rest of the basket, putting in the geraniums, marigolds, mimulus and calceolaria in that order.

5. Gently firm down the compost around the plants and level off the surface so that it is just below the rim. Add the fertilizer tablet, if used. Water thoroughly.

MAINTENANCE

Keep well watered and cut out any straggly stems.

Petunia Pie

*W*HAT A SPLENDID sight this is against the black and white of the old building! The various shades of pink create a fresh, lively picture that will remain colourful for a very long time. It is the rich topping of petunias, with their strong colours and velvety texture, that makes this display so attractive, but all the plants contribute to the overall success, including the colourful sweeps of the lobelias and the verbena and the dainty flowers of the geraniums.

INGREDIENTS

1 pink zonal geranium (*Pelargonium* 'Highfield Pink') **(A)**
3 mixed-coloured petunias (*Petunia* Mixed) **(B)**
1 bush fuchsia (*Fuchsia* 'Royal Velvet') **(C)**
1 trailing fuchsia (*Fuchsia* 'Swingtime') **(D)**
1 calceolaria (*Calceolaria* 'Sunshine') **(E)**
2 pink cascade geraniums (*Pelargonium* 'Pink Mini Cascade') **(F)**
5 mixed lobelias (*Lobelia* 'Cascade Mixed') **(G)**
1 plectranthus (*Plectranthus coleoides* 'Variegatus') **(H)**
1 pink verbena (*Verbena* 'Sissinghurst') **(I)**
1 trailing petunia (*Petunia* 'Purple Wave') **(J)**

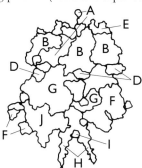

CONTAINER

45cm (18in) plastic-covered wire basket

MATERIALS

Liner
General-purpose compost
Water-retaining granules
Slow-release fertilizer tablet or granules

POSITION

This is a heavy basket and must be well supported in a sunny position that is protected from the wind.

PLANTING

1. Plant up the basket in spring but keep it in a conservatory or greenhouse until the frosts have passed.

2. Hang the basket at a convenient height or support it on a large flowerpot. Line the basket and trim off any excess.

3. Three-quarters fill the baskets with a general-purpose compost and mix in the water-retaining granules and also the fertilizer granules, if you are using them.

4. Make two holes in the liner and plant the plectranthus and the verbena. Continue to fill the basket with compost, pressing it down lightly around the roots of the plants.

5. Plant the top, beginning with the zonal geranium and then adding the pelargoniums and the fuchsias. Next plant the cascade geraniums and tuck in the lobelias around them. Finally, plant the calceolaria for a splash of yellow.

6. Gently firm down the compost around all the plants and level off the surface just below the rim of the basket. Add the fertilizer tablet if you are using one. Water thoroughly.

MAINTENANCE

Water regularly. Remove any dead flowers and straggly stems.

Variegated Delight

NASTURTIUMS ARE BETTER plants than they are often given credit for. They come in a range of rich colours, all with a velvety texture that enhances the warm tones. The colours in this variety contrast beautifully with the cream variegations in the leaves, the whole creating a ball of great beauty. These nasturtiums are not difficult to maintain and can be easily raised from a packet of seed, making it one of the cheapest displays to create. Save the seeds and it will be even cheaper next year.

INGREDIENTS

6 variegated nasturtiums (*Tropaeolum majus* 'Alaska Mixed') **(A)**

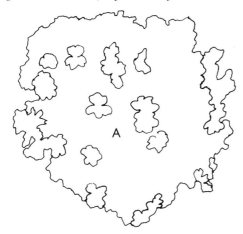

CONTAINER

30cm (12in) plastic-covered wire basket

MATERIALS

Liner
General-purpose compost
Water-retaining granules
Slow-release fertilizer tablet or granules

POSITION

A sunny position would be best, but the basket will take a little light shade.

PLANTING

1. Nasturtiums will be killed by frost, so do not be in too much of a hurry to hang this basket outside. It can be made up in spring and kept inside until early summer.

2. Line the basket and trim off any liner that protrudes above the rim of the basket. Part fill the basket with a general-purpose compost and add the water-retaining granules. If you are using them, the fertilizer granules can also be added at this stage. Mix them both well into the compost.

3. Fill the rest of the basket with the compost and gently firm down. Insert the six plants, spacing them evenly around the basket. Alternatively, nasturtium seeds can be sown directly into the basket in early spring to save transplanting. Plant a couple of extra seeds to ensure that enough germinate. You can always thin them out later.

4. Firm the compost down gently around the plants or over the seeds. Level it off so that the final level is about 2.5cm (1in) below the rim of the basket. If you are using a fertilizer tablet rather than granules, now is the time to push it into the soil.

5. Water thoroughly either by standing the basket in a bowl of water or by using a watering can.

MAINTENANCE

Water regularly and remove any dead flowers when necessary.

Beautiful Begonia

*B*EGONIAS SEEM TO *be the aristocrats of the hanging basket world. Unlike many of the airy plants that are frequently used, they have a solidity and substance about them, and yet they still hang gracefully. The begonia in this basket has flowers of a lovely golden-yellow flushed with apricot, and this latter colour helps combine the begonia with the pinks of the petunias and the busy lizzies. The lobelia and Swan River daisy make a good fringe to the display, while the fuchsia forms a brilliant red tassel.*

INGREDIENTS

1 golden begonia (*Begonia* × *tuberhybrida* 'Apricot Cascade') **(A)**
2 double petunias (*Petunia* 'Delight Mixed') **(B)**
3 mixed busy lizzies (*Impatiens*) **(C)**
1 trailing fuchsia (*Fuchsia* 'Marinka') **(D)**
1 pale blue lobelia (*Lobelia* 'Light Blue Basket') **(E)**
1 Swan River daisy (*Brachycome iberidifolia*) **(F)**

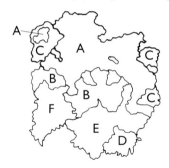

CONTAINER

35cm (14in) plastic-covered wire basket

MATERIALS

Liner
Lime-free (ericaceous) compost
Water-retaining granules
Slow-release fertilizer tablet or granules

POSITION

Although this display looks best in a sunny position, it should be sited so that it is not in the hot midday sun.

PLANTING

1. Plant up this basket in the spring and move it outside in the early summer, once the last frosts have finished.

2. Balance the empty basket on a large flowerpot or hang it at a convenient height while you work. Line the basket with your preferred liner, trimming it if necessary.

3. Using a lime-free compost because begonias prefer acid conditions, three-quarters fill the basket. Mix in the water-retaining granules and also fertilizer granules if you want to use them. Fill up the rest of the basket and compress the compost slightly.

4. Plant the begonia first, taking care not to break any of the brittle stems. Next plant the two busy lizzies at the back of the display, then add the petunias. Next plant the fuchsia, the Swan River daisy and, finally, the third busy lizzie and the lobelia.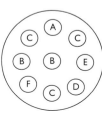

5. Gently firm down the compost between the plants and level off the surface so that it is about 2.5cm (1in) below the rim of the basket. At this point, insert the fertilizer tablet if you are using one.

6. Water thoroughly.

MAINTENANCE

Water regularly. There is no need to feed if you used a slow-release fertilizer.

Pretty Pansies

EVEN IF YOU use only one type of plant in an arrangement, you do not have to use a single variety. Although this display is made up entirely of pansies, there are so many different types that the basket could almost be composed of different plants, and the various colours combine to make an attractive, cheerful medley. Pansies are widely available and are easy enough to grow, which means that you can always have some in reserve to replace any that stop flowering or become too straggly.

INGREDIENTS

8 mixed pansies (*Viola*) **(A)**

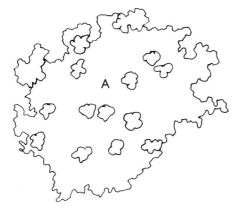

CONTAINER

30cm (12in) plastic-covered wire basket

MATERIALS

Liner
General-purpose compost
Water-retaining granules
Slow-release fertilizer tablet or granules

POSITION

Pansies do not like too hot a position, so place the basket in light shade or at least where it will be out of the sun during the hottest part of the day.

PLANTING

1. Pansies are hardy, so this basket can be planted and hung outside in the spring, unlike most other summer baskets. It is also possible to use winter-flowering pansies to create a similar display for the duller months of the year.

2. Stand the basket on a bucket or large flowerpot to make it easier to handle. Alternatively hang it at a convenient working height. Place a liner in the basket.

3. Part fill the basket with a general-purpose compost and mix into this the water-retaining granules. If you are using fertilizer granules, this is also the time to add these. Winter pansies will not need either of these. Mix the ingredients together.

4. Fill up the basket with compost and gently press it down. Plant the pansies, spacing them evenly around the basket. To get a better coverage on the sides of the basket, cut holes in the liner and insert some plants through the holes.

5. Gently firm down the compost around the plants and level off the surface so that it is about 2.5cm (1in) below the rim of the basket. If you are using a fertilizer tablet, now is the time to add it to the top of the compost.

6. Stand the basket in a bowl of water so that the compost is thoroughly soaked.

MAINTENANCE

Water regularly and remove any dead flowers as necessary.

Red Eye

*A*LTHOUGH THIS IS *generally a bright basket, the scarlet ivy-leaved geraniums stand out like beacons, immediately drawing the eye. Bright red always looks good against dark green, especially a shiny dark green as here. In spite of the dominant geraniums, the other plants have an important part to play in the overall picture, especially the fuchsias, which echo the colour of the geraniums. The remaining plants soften the composition around the edges and make the arrangement an attractive whole.*

INGREDIENTS

1 scarlet ivy-leaved geranium (*Pelargonium* 'Lily Marlene') (**A**)
1 red and purple fuchsia (*Fuchsia* 'Indian Maid') (**B**)
1 lime green helichrysum (*Helichrysum petiolare* 'Limelight') (**C**)
1 blue petunia (*Petunia* 'Lavender Storm') (**D**)
3 mixed busy lizzies (*Impatiens*) (**E**)
1 deep pink fuchsia (*Fuchsia* 'Jack Acland') (**F**)
2 mixed lobelias (*Lobelia* 'Cascade Mixed') (**G**)

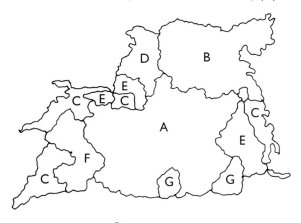

CONTAINER

35cm (14in) plastic-covered wire basket

MATERIALS

Liner
General-purpose compost
Water-retaining granules
Slow-release fertilizer tablet or granules

POSITION

Hang this basket in a sunny position, although it can be placed where it misses the hot midday sun.

PLANTING

1. Plant up the basket in spring, but keep it in a conservatory or greenhouse until no more frosts are likely.

2. Support the basket in a bucket or large flowerpot or hang it at a convenient height while you work. Put in the liner, trimming it to size if necessary.

3. Three-quarters fill the basket with a general-purpose compost and mix in the water-retaining granules. If you want to use fertilizer granules, these can also be added now, too.

4. Cut two holes in the liner and plant the lobelias through into the compost. Continue to add compost, pressing it down lightly around the lobelia roots.

5. Start the main planting with the helichrysum in the centre and then add the two fuchsias and the geranium. Next plant the petunia, followed by the three busy lizzies.

6. Gently firm down the compost between the plants and level off the surface just below the rim of the basket. Add the fertilizer tablet if you wish to use one. Water thoroughly.

MAINTENANCE

Do not allow the compost to dry out and deadhead as necessary.

Avalanche

*I*N THIS BASKET *it is not so much the bright reds and purples that catch the eye as the white, and the way in which the lobelias have been used really makes their flowers stand out, looking for all the world like a white avalanche spreading across the basket. This is helped by the way in which the display has been sited in a slightly shaded position and against a dark background. It will show up particularly well in the evening, just as the light is fading, making it a dramatic basket to hang close to where you might have your evening meal.*

INGREDIENTS

1 red zonal geranium (*Pelargonium* 'Dryden') **(A)**
2 purple petunias (*Petunia* 'Carpet Mixed') **(B)**
2 trailing nasturtiums (*Tropaeolum majus*) **(C)**
2 white lobelias (*Lobelia* 'White Cascade') **(D)**

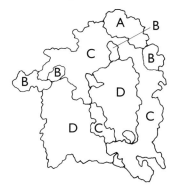

CONTAINER

35cm (14in) plastic-covered wire basket

MATERIALS

Liner
General-purpose compost
Water-retaining granules
Slow-release fertilizer tablet or granules

POSITION

Place this basket in a sunny or semi-shaded position,
preferably against a dark background.

PLANTING

1. Although you can prepare this basket in spring, do not place it outside until early summer, after the last of the frosts.

2. Hang the basket at a convenient height or, if the plants are not already trailing, support it on a bucket or large flower-pot while you work. Fit a liner into the basket, trimming off any that protrudes above the rim.

3. Using a general-purpose compost, three-quarters fill the basket, adding the water-retaining granules and, if you wish, the fertilizer granules. Mix them well into the compost.

4. Make a slit at one side of the liner and push one of the lobelias through into the compost. Continue filling the basket until the compost reaches the rim, pressing it down lightly around the roots of the lobelia.

5. Now add the rest of the plants, starting with the geranium. Plant the two nasturtiums, followed by the two petunias. Finally, place the second lobelia so that it forms a visual link with the first.

6. Gently firm down the compost around the plants and level off the surface just below the rim. Add a fertilizer tablet if you have not already added granules. Water thoroughly.

MAINTENANCE

Water regularly and deadhead when necessary. Keep the basket tidy and maintain its shape by trimming off any wayward stems as they appear.

Cacti Collection

*T*HIS IS A BASKET with a difference. Cacti are not something that you would immediately associate with hanging baskets, but as this arrangement proves, they can be very effective indeed. Almost any of the smaller cacti can be used as they usually associate very well together. In addition to being attractive to look at, they have the advantage that they do not require watering and feeding as frequently as baskets filled with more conventional plants. The effect is not difficult to achieve and will certainly prove a talking point.

INGREDIENTS

A collection of cacti (A–H)

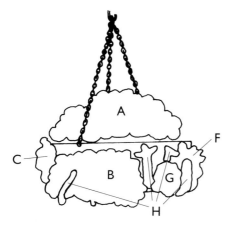

CONTAINER

30cm (12in) plastic-covered wire basket

MATERIALS

Neutral-coloured liner
Lime-free (ericaceous) compost
Extra horticultural grit
White chippings

POSITION

This basket needs careful siting as it looks best against a plain background. It should be placed in a warm, sunny situation.

PLANTING

1. Assemble a collection of cacti from your local nursery or garden centre, looking carefully at what is available and choosing those with contrasting or sympathetic shapes.

2. Prop up the basket on a large flowerpot or hang it at a convenient height while you work. Insert a neutral-coloured liner; one made from coir fibre would be ideal.

3. The compost must be very well drained, so mix 1 part grit to 3 parts soil-based compost or 1 part grit to 2 parts soil-less compost. There is no need to add extra fertilizer or water-retaining granules.

4. Part fill the container and insert the lower cacti through holes in the liner. Continue to fill the basket, cutting holes and planting the higher layers of cacti as you go. If the cacti have spines or are delicate, wrap a piece of folded paper or cloth around them so that you can handle them safely. When you reach the top of the basket gently firm down the compost.

5. Plant the cacti that are to go on the surface of the basket and level off the compost. Top dress with stone chippings or gravel before watering with tepid water.

MAINTENANCE

Water only while the plants are in active growth. Use tepid water and allow the compost to dry out between waterings. Either use a special cactus fertilizer or a general one, feeding once a month during the growing season.

Spider Fountain

IF YOU WANT a simple but effective basket, this could be the design for you. It consists of a spider plant, which is normally seen as a houseplant, surrounded by two tiers of different coloured busy lizzies. Spider plants are useful additions to a hanging basket, and an interesting design can be made by just using several of them, without any other plants. This fountain effect has been created by having the spider plant erupt from a mound of busy lizzies, while the lower ones are a lighter colour as if they are the splashing water.

INGREDIENTS

1 spider plant (*Chlorophytum comosum* 'Vittatum') **(A)**
8 light pink busy lizzies (*Impatiens*) **(B)**
4 dark pink busy lizzies (*Impatiens*) **(C)**

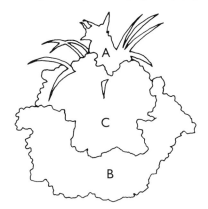

CONTAINER

30cm (12in) plastic-covered wire basket

MATERIALS

Liner
General-purpose compost
Water-retaining granules
Slow-release fertilizer tablet or granules

POSITION

This display will tolerate quite a bit of shade and is best placed so that it does not get the sun during the hottest part of the day.

PLANTING

1. Neither of these plants is hardy. They will easily be killed in a frost, so wait until the frosts have passed before you think about hanging the basket outside.

2. Hang the basket at a convenient height or support it in a bucket or flowerpot while you work. Line the basket with your chosen liner and trim off any protruding above the rim.

3. Part fill the basket with a general-purpose compost. Add some water-retaining granules and mix in. If you want to use fertilizer granules, these should also be added now.

4. Cut four holes through the liner, spacing them evenly, and add a circle of the paler busy lizzies. Add more compost, pushing it around the roots of the plants. Cut another circle of holes, spacing them between and above the first group. Plant the other paler busy lizzies.

5. Finish filling the basket to the brim with compost. Plant the spider plant in the centre of the basket and then add the darker busy lizzies around it.

6. Firm down the compost around each plant and level off the surface just below the rim of the basket. Add a fertilizer tablet if you wish, and water thoroughly.

MAINTENANCE

Water regularly and deadhead the busy lizzies.

Herb Basket

*H*ERBS ARE OFTEN *grown in containers and there is no reason why they should not also be grown in hanging baskets, as long as they are not so high that you cannot reach to pick them. This silver-leaved curry plant and variegated apple mint contrast beautifully with the red and yellow nasturtiums. Also tucked in on the surface of the basket is a carpet of thyme. The nasturtium flowers and leaves can be used in salads and garnishes, while the others can be used as flavourings.*

INGREDIENTS

1 variegated apple mint (*Mentha suaveolens* 'Variegata') **(A)**
3 curry plants (*Helichrysum italicum*) **(B)**
3 thymes (*Thymus serpyllum*) **(C)**
8 mixed nasturtiums (*Tropaeolum majus*) **(D)**

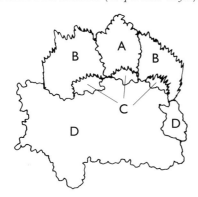

CONTAINER

30cm (12in) plastic-covered wire basket

MATERIALS

Liner
General-purpose compost
Water-retaining granules
Slow-release fertilizer tablet or granules

POSITION

Hang this basket in the sun, but do not place it too high from the ground.

PLANTING

1. Although mint, thyme and curry plant are hardy, nasturtiums are tender, and the display should be kept inside or not made up until after the risk of frost has passed.

2. To make it easier to work, hang the basket at a convenient height or support it on a bucket or flowerpot. Put in a liner and trim off any that protrudes above the rim of the basket.

3. Three-quarters fill the basket with a general-purpose compost. Mix into this the water-retaining granules and, if you want to use them, a quantity of fertilizer granules.

4. Make eight holes through the liner and plant the nasturtiums into the compost. Continue to fill the basket with compost and firm down.

5. Plant the mint in the centre of the basket, spacing the three curry plants evenly around it. In between, plant the thymes so that they form a carpet over the surface.

6. Level off the compost, firming it down around the plants. The final surface should be just below the rim of the basket. Bury the fertilizer tablet if you are using one, then water thoroughly.

MAINTENANCE

Water the basket once a day and remove any dead nasturtium flowers as they occur. Cut back the curry plant if it gets too tall for the basket.

Canned Plants

*M*OST GARDENERS STICK *to the conventional hanging basket made from wire or plastic, but, with a little imagination, it is possible to use a variety of other hanging containers, including the mop bucket that is used for this arrangement. The bucket is plain and simple, and you should avoid anything that is too over-the-top or the display may well look ludicrous. The pewter-mottled foliage of the heuchera echoes the colour of the bucket, while the creeping Jenny and the nemisia provide movement and interest.*

INGREDIENTS

1 pewter-leafed heuchera (*Heuchera* 'Pewter Moon') **(A)**
1 golden creeping Jenny (*Lysimachia nummularia* 'Aurea') **(B)**
1 nemisia (*Nemisia caerulea*) **(C)**

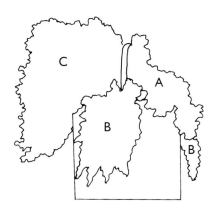

CONTAINER

Weathered mop bucket

MATERIALS

General-purpose compost
Water-retaining granules
Slow-release fertilizer tablet or granules

POSITION

Either a sunny or a lightly shaded position will be suitable for this bucket. Too much shade, however, will draw the nemisia.

PLANTING

1. The best way to plant this particular container is to use plants that are in individual pots, which should simply be placed in the bucket. A container of this size will weigh a lot if it is filled with moist compost. Smaller or lighter containers can be used more in the manner of a conventional basket and filled in the normal way.

2. Whatever kind of container you use must have holes in the bottom so that excess water can drain away.

3. Fill the container with a general-purpose compost, adding water-retaining granules if you are worried that the compost is likely to dry out. Fertilizer granules can also be added to the compost at this stage.

4. Start with the golden creeping Jenny, which should be planted in the centre. Then plant the nemisia and the heuchera at either end.

5. Firm down the compost and level off the surface about 2.5cm (1in) below the rim of the container. If you are using one, push a fertilizer tablet into the compost at this stage. Water thoroughly.

MAINTENANCE

Keep the container watered and, if you have not used a slow-release fertilizer, apply a liquid feed every two weeks. If you leave the plants in pots, it is a simple task to swap plants occasionally to provide continuous interest.

Bright Begonias

*T*HE BRIGHT YELLOW *begonia immediately draws the eye in this display. It contrasts well with the purples of the petunias and the fiery oranges of the nasturtiums, while the purple-blue of the lobelia enhances the deepening shadow beneath the basket. The shape of the basket is well disguised, with the begonia providing a smooth dome at the top, which is emphasized by the flowing lines of the nasturtiums and petunias as they tumble over the side of the basket and by the upward sweep of the geraniums.*

INGREDIENTS

1 nasturtium (*Tropaeolum majus*) **(A)**
2 petunias (*Petunia* 'Mirage Reflections') **(B)**
1 begonia (*Begonia* × *tuberhybrida* 'Gold Cascade') **(C)**
3 lobelias (*Lobelia* 'Sapphire') **(D)**
1 ivy-leaved geranium (*Pelargonium* 'Hederinum') **(E)**

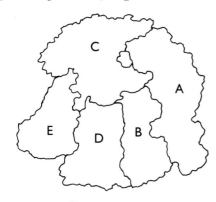

CONTAINER

35cm (14in) plastic-covered wire container

MATERIALS

Liner
Lime-free (ericaceous) compost
Water-retaining granules
Slow-release fertilizer tablet or granules

POSITION

A sunny or a semi-shaded position would be suitable.

PLANTING

1. Place the basket on a bucket to make it easier to handle. Line the basket with a liner of your choice, but preferably a water-retaining one.

2. Because begonias prefer acid conditions, part fill the basket with lime-free compost. Add some water-retaining granules and mix them into the compost. Add the fertilizer granules at this stage, too, if you wish.

3. Cut three slits in the liner and insert the lobelias through the liner into the compost. Continue to fill the container until it is nearly full and press down the compost lightly.

4. Plant the begonia towards the centre back with a petunia to its right and the geranium to its left. In front, plant the nasturtium and another petunia, both slightly to the right so that the begonia will grow forwards into the gap.

5. Firm down the compost until the final surface is about 2.5cm (1in) below the rim of the hanging basket.

6. Place a fertilizer tablet in the compost if wished, then stand the basket in a bucket of water to give it a thorough soaking.

MAINTENANCE

Water daily if necessary. If a slow-release fertilizer has not been used, add a liquid feed to the water once a week. Deadhead regularly. Cut off any straggly stems. All the plants are long-flowering so there should be no need to replace any of them.

Autumn Glow

*T*HIS DELIGHTFUL DISPLAY *is made of plants that simply glow with vibrant autumn colours, and the contrasting browns, red and yellows make an attractive display. Most of these plants are rarely seen in hanging baskets; they are perennials and are more at home in the herbaceous or mixed border. In spite of its unusual quality, it is not a difficult basket to create, and all the ingredients can be used again in other baskets or planted in the border.*

INGREDIENTS

1 variegated carex (*Carex hachijoensis* 'Evergold') **(A)**
1 purple tellima (*Tellima grandiflora* 'Rubra') **(B)**
1 epimedium (*Epimedium* × *versicolor* 'Sulphureum') **(C)**
1 young enkianthus (*Enkianthus campanulatus*) **(D)**
3 heathers (*Calluna vulgaris* 'Silver Knight') **(E)**
1 variegated grass (*Hakonechloa macra* 'Alboaurea') **(F)**
3 variegated ivies (*Hedera helix*) **(G)**

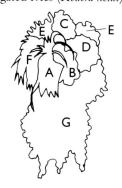

CONTAINER

30cm (12in) plastic-coated wire basket

MATERIALS

Liner
Lime-free (ericaceous) compost

POSITION

A sunny place. If possible, site the basket so that it is viewed from the front against a dark green background.

PLANTING

1. Plant up in late summer, using small plants, except for the ivies which should already be mature and trailing.

2. Hang the basket at a convenient height or support it on an empty bucket while you work. Line the basket with a liner of your choice, trimming it to size if necessary.

3. Half fill the container with compost. It should be lime-free because heathers need an acid compost. Make holes at the front and sides of the basket and plant the three ivies through them. Continue to fill the basket with compost, firming it down as you go.

4. Plant the three heathers at the back and the enkianthus in the middle of the basket. Follow this up with the epimedium to one side and the tellima in the centre front. Tuck in the hakonechloa and carex on the other side.

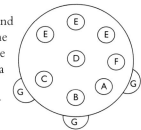

5. Firm down the compost, levelling it off about 2.5cm (1in) below the rim of the basket. Stand it in a bucket of water to soak.

MAINTENANCE

Being an autumn display, most of the plants are not growing very fast, if at all, and therefore do not need a great deal of moisture and only the occasional feed. Water to keep the compost just moist and apply a liquid feed about once every three weeks.

Cabbage White

ORNAMENTAL CABBAGES ARE *increasingly used in containers for winter decoration, so why not in hanging baskets too? This unusual display is certain to be noticed and appreciated. The creamy colours of the cabbage are well complemented by the variegations in the ivies, and the squat shape of the cabbages contrasts with the upward thrust of the heathers and the downward sweep of the ivies, creating an altogether satisfying picture. It is an easy display to create and needs virtually no maintenance.*

INGREDIENTS

4 white ornamental kales (Cabbage 'White Northern Lights') **(A)**
3 heathers (*Erica carnea* 'Springwood White') **(B)**
6 three-coloured ivies (*Hedera helix*) **(C)**

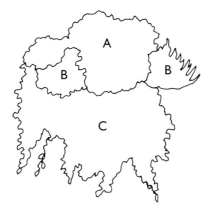

CONTAINER

30cm (12in) plastic-covered wire container

MATERIALS

Liner
Lime-free (ericaceous) compost

POSITION

Any position will do, although the white cabbage will help lighten up a dark corner. Cabbages smell, so do not put the basket in a porch or near a regular walkway.

PLANTING

1. Prepare this basket in the autumn and hang it elsewhere until it is required.

2. Support the basket on an empty bucket while you work. Choose a liner and place it in the basket, trimming it to size if necessary.

3. Fill the basket with compost firming it gently. Start by planting the three heathers, each behind one of the chains. If you leave these until last they may be difficult to get into position. Next plant the central cabbage, followed by the three outer ones. These should be planted slightly deep so that the overall effect is dome-shaped. Finally, tuck in the ivies between the other plants. If you use more developed ivies, you may not need so many to get the same effect.

4. Gently firm down the compost around the plants and level it off about 2.5cm (1in) below the rim.

5. Stand the completed basket in a bucket of water to give it a good soaking.

MAINTENANCE

This display is not a growing one and so its demands on water and nutrients are low. It does not need constant watering and in most winters will get enough moisture from natural rain, unless, of course, it is under cover. Water to keep the compost just moist. There should be enough nutrients in the compost, so do not feed. The display needs little attention other than the removal of any dead or dying cabbage leaves.

Winter Mixture

COLOUR IN HANGING baskets during the winter months is at a premium, but this delightful arrangement offers just that. Unfortunately, however, there is a price to pay, for both the cyclamen and the Jerusalem cherry are tender. This does not matter if the basket hangs within the protection of a porch or against a warm wall and is brought inside during cold weather. The cyclamen can always be replaced. The pansy is not yet in flower but will help to prolong the life of the basket.

INGREDIENTS

1 Jerusalem cherry (*Solanum pseudocapsicum*) **(A)**
2 florist's cyclamen (*Cyclamen*) **(B)**
1 yellow primula (*Primula*) **(C)**
1 blue pansy (*Viola* 'True Blue') **(D)**
1 winter euonymus (*Euonymus* 'Ovatus Aureus') **(E)**
4 plain and variegated ivies (*Hedera helix*) **(F)**

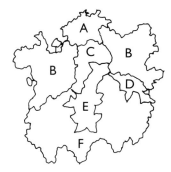

CONTAINER

30cm (12in) plastic-covered wire basket

MATERIALS

Liner
General-purpose compost

POSITION

A covered porch or the protection of a warm wall is needed.
Do not put in an open position where frost or cold winds
will kill the cyclamen and the Jerusalem cherry.

PLANTING

1. Plant this basket as the cyclamen become available and put outside when the weather is mild.

2. Support the basket on a bucket or large flowerpot while you work. Line the basket with your preferred liner and trim off any excess.

3. Fill the basket with compost. There is no need to add slow-release fertilizer or water-retaining granules as the plants are not in full growth.

4. Start by planting the Jerusalem cherry and follow this with the two cyclamen. Next plant the primula and the pansy, surrounding them with the four ivies, followed by the euonymus in the front. Arrange the ivy so that it hangs down naturally.

5. Gently press the compost down around the various plants and level off the surface so that it is about 2.5cm (1in) below the rim of the basket.

6. Water the basket thoroughly from below by standing it in a bowl of water or from above with a watering can.

MAINTENANCE

Take care that you do not over-water this arrangement; water it only when the compost begins to dry out. If the cyclamen are caught by frost or finish flowering, replace them with new plants.

Pansies Galore

*T*HE USE OF *a single type and colour of flower can be very effective. The simplicity of the scheme often makes it pleasing and restful to the eye and, therefore, easy to appreciate. This can work at any time of year, but in winter, when the choice of plants is naturally restricted, using one plant is a sensible practice. Pansies are especially versatile: they can be used alone or they can be mixed with other varieties. They also have the advantage of being available at most times of the year.*

INGREDIENTS

3 yellow pansies (*Viola* 'Yellow Blotch') **(A)**

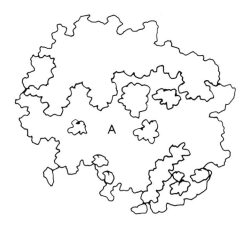

CONTAINER

20cm (8in) hanging pot

MATERIALS

Liner
General-purpose compost
Small stones or gravel

POSITION

This display can be hung in a sunny or
a lightly shaded position.

PLANTING

1. Autumn is a good time to make up this display, while the plants are quite small, but it need not be hung in position until the plants are in flower.

2. Unlike baskets, this pot is flat-bottomed and so can be easily worked on while it is standing on a table.

3. Place a layer of gravel or small stones in the bottom of the pot to improve drainage, then fill the pot with a general-purpose compost. Press it down lightly.

4. Plant the three pansies, spacing them evenly around the pot. Gently firm down the compost around the roots and level off the surface of the compost so that it is just below the top of the pot.

5. Water thoroughly by standing the pot in a bucket of water, then pour away any surplus water in the drip tray if the container has one.

MAINTENANCE

This display is virtually maintenance free. Unless it is under the cover of a porch or eaves, it should get enough rainwater to keep it going. Look out for warm, dry spells, when the compost may dry out. If the pot has a drip tray, empty it regularly so that water does not stagnate in it. Feed once a month with a weak liquid feed. Remove any dead flowers. Do not keep the plants too compact; let a few shoots hang over the edge of the pot to disguise its harsh lines.

Choosing a Hanging Basket

THERE IS A SURPRISINGLY wide range of hanging baskets available, although it must be said that there is not a great deal to chose between them. If a display is designed correctly, little, if any, of the basket should show, so all you need is a frame to hold everything together. As long as it is strong enough to do the job, it does not matter what it looks like and so there is really no disadvantage in choosing the least expensive. Before you buy, however, there are a few points that you should consider.

Most hanging baskets follow the same basic design. They consist simply of a wire framework, shaped into half a sphere.

A cool design, which blends well with the mellow stone wall. The colours are sympathetic to each other, creating a subtle image.

The standard sizes are 25cm (10in), 30cm (12in), 35cm (14in), 40cm (16in) and 45cm (18in), which is the diameter of the rim. They are supported by three chains, which join together and hook onto a bracket or some other support. Because the wire struts of the basket are widely spaced, some form of lining is required to prevent the compost from falling out. There is a wide range of different materials for these, and these are discussed below. In most baskets the plants can be inserted both into the top of the basket and also into the sides, through holes or slits cut in the liner. In a well-designed display, neither the basket itself nor its liner can be seen.

TYPES OF BASKET

The most commonly seen baskets are those made from strong wire covered with a green plastic coating. The wire is usually relatively thin and, being green, is not very noticeable. Some baskets have loops that extend above the rim of the basket, but this does not seem to confer any real advantage and is probably not worth any extra expense involved.

Some baskets are made of plastic, and these usually have quite thick struts that tend to show more. Plastic degrades in the open, and baskets made of it should be replaced if they become brittle to avoid a disaster. Plastic baskets are available in several colours, but green is likely to be the best as it will help the basket merge with the foliage. White will often remain visible, even through quite dense foliage.

There are an increasing number of 'forged' baskets, which are made by blacksmiths from broad iron bars. These are sometimes just painted, but some kinds are dipped in plastic, and the coating has the effect of making them last longer.

These baskets, which look attractive, are much more expensive than the plastic-coated wire ones, and although they will last a long time, the extra expense for the appearance alone is not necessarily money well spent, because once the basket is full of plants you should not be able to see much of the blacksmith's art. They are best used in designs that involve plants only on the surface of the basket so that the framework shows.

In recent years a new type of plastic basket has been introduced. In their simplest form they are similar in shape to the traditional basket except that they are formed from a solid sheet of plastic. The advantage is that you do not need a liner, but the disadvantage is that you can plant only in the top and not in the sides.

A more expensive form of this type of basket has been developed, and in these a water reservoir is incorporated in the bottom of the basket so that the frequency of watering is reduced. This system can work well in warm weather, but in rainy conditions the plants can easily become swamped with water, much to their detriment. The principle is that the water is conducted via a wick from the bottom of the pot up into the compost. The reservoir is kept topped up with water via a tube that emerges at the surface of the basket. When the basket is hanging way above your head, it is not the easiest of things to find the tube and pour water through it. Nor is it easy to know when too much water has been put in or when it has run out.

Although they were developed mainly for indoor use, some people use hanging plastic pots rather than baskets. These have a drip tray to prevent water falling on the carpet, but they can be used outside – again, only for planting in the top. Other disadvantages of these pots are that their size is limited and, if the tray retains too much water, the plants will become waterlogged. Another problem is that plastic pots generally use strips of plastic rather than chains as a support, and these are not strong, particularly after a couple of years in bright sunlight, and could break. They also look clumsy and very rarely hold enough plants to make a proper display.

Winter is a difficult time to grow hanging baskets, but these pansies help create a cheerful scene during the bleak months.

All the types described above are also available as half-baskets. These are not suspended on chains, but hung on hooks or screwed directly to the wall. Apart from their shape and method of attachment, they are identical to the standard baskets, in both construction and their need for liners. You should bear in mind that because they are attached to the wall, water can leak out of the basket and trickle down the surface, possibly staining it.

A recent development has been the use of long polythene sleeves. These are hung in the same way as baskets, but the plants are planted all the way up the tube, in slits made in the plastic, creating a hanging column of flowers. In a way, this is little more than a vertical growing bag, but it can be very successful. The tubes must be well planted so that the polythene does not show.

It is possible to make your own baskets, and before the advent of cheap, mass-produced, metal and plastic ones, many people did so. The simplest way is to take a 30 × 30cm (12 × 12in) piece of waterproof plywood and 20 lengths of wood, each 35cm (14in) long and 3.5 × 2.5cm (1½ × 1in) or 2.5 × 2.5cm (1 × 1in) in cross-section, and make these up into a slat-sided box. Drill holes in the corners of the plywood and through both ends of the lengths of wood. Tie knots into the ends of four lengths (60cm/24in each) of nylon cord and thread the untied end through the holes in the plywood base. Then pass them through the battens, laying two opposite ones in one direction and the next two at right angles to these, in a 'log cabin-type' construction, so that each side is made up alternately of a batten and then a space. Add more battens if you want the basket to be deeper. Pull the strings together above the basket, check that the basket will hang level and knot the ends together. This kind of basket will last longer if it is made from wood treated with a preservative, but do not use creosote, which will kill the plants.

While it is undoubtedly satisfying to make your own basket in this way, it is almost certain to be more expensive than simply buying a wire basket unless you already have

Summer pansies in a plastic hanging basket. This solid basket contains a reservoir of water which cuts down the need for watering.

some suitable scraps of wood lying around that you can use.

A final possibility is to use a ready-made container. Perhaps the most obvious would be a wicker basket. If it is disposable then it can be filled with compost in the same way as a wire basket, but to increase its lifespan, the plants can be arranged inside the basket without taking them out of their pots. Many other types of container can be used. In one of the recipes, for example, a mop bucket has been used, but any bucket or similar container could be brought into service. Watch out for weight, however, because metal containers will invariably be very heavy when they are filled with moist compost. You could occasionally use a fun container, such as an old boot, but be careful not to overdo it as this kind of novelty can quickly become boring rather than amusing.

SUPPORTS

Most conventionally shaped baskets are hung on three chains. Each chain is attached to the rim of the basket at one end and drawn together onto a ring at the other. The chain is usually metal and will last for years without weakening. However, it is worth checking for any weakness before you hang a basket.

Petunias, busy lizzies and fuchsias are three popular choices for hanging baskets. They can be used singly or mixed with other plants.

Baskets are usually hung from brackets attached to a wall. Garden centres and nurseries carry quite a wide range of sizes and decorative finishes, although metal is the preferred material, simply because it is the most durable. Make certain that the bracket is securely fixed to the wall. It can usually be screwed straight into the brickwork, but if the surface of the

In a design like this it does not matter what basket or liner you use, as neither will be seen under the welter of flowers and foliage.

wall is uneven, first attach a wooden batten to the wall and then screw the bracket to this. Each year, before you hang up a basket, check that the bracket is still secure, and examine those held with wooden battens especially carefully to make certain that the wood has not deteriorated.

The plastic brackets and stays that you find are not as strong as metal chains and are likely to deteriorate in sunlight. They are initially cheaper than metal ones, but they will need replacing at frequent intervals, which makes them more expensive in the longer term. Do not trust old, brittle ones, because you might find the basket on the floor or, worse, on someone's head.

Most of the available brackets involve some sort of scrollwork, ending in a curl on which the basket is hung. If this is almost a complete circle, there is usually no danger of the basket falling off, but if it is open there is the possibility that the basket may be knocked or blown off. To be safe, use a length of wire to secure the basket in position once it has been hung up.

Normally, the chains are attached direct to the supporting bracket by means of a loop or hook. It is, however, possible to buy or make some form of device for lifting or lowering the basket so that it is easy to water and maintain. This can be done with a simple pulley, but the need to have a rope to pull it up and down means that the area around the basket begins to look like the deck of a sailing ship. An alternative method is to use a special device that includes a counterbalancing spring, so that the basket will remain at whatever level it is set. This is a neat gadget, no bigger than a pulley block, but with only a single wire coming down to the basket.

You need not be restricted to house walls when it comes to displaying a hanging basket. Baskets can be suspended from porches or any overhanging part of the house or outbuildings. They can also be hung from boundary walls or fences. Another possibility is to hang them from poles firmly planted in the ground. You could, for example, use poles to line a path or to decorate the edge of a patio. Another idea is to incorporate them into the structure of an arbour or pergola.

Some baskets can be bought already mounted on stands. In some cases there are two or more baskets, one above the other, with the pole passing through the lower ones. Make certain that the base is wide and heavy enough to prevent the stand being knocked or blown over.

LINERS

Apart from those baskets with solid plastic walls, all other types of basket will need lining to prevent the compost falling through or being washed out. There are several types of commercially produced liners on the market or you can make your own.

The first of the home-made liners is also the oldest – moss. Sphagnum moss can be bought at most of the larger garden centres and nurseries as well as many florists. It gives a rough but natural finish to the side of the basket, and often bulges slightly, so hiding the metal struts. For many people this is still the preferred method, even though there are now many easier alternatives.

The second home-made method is simply to line the basket with a sheet of polythene and to trim it off level with the rim of the basket. Any polythene can be used, although black is preferable, making this a cost-free as well as easy option.

Of the ready-made versions, one of the most popular is that made from fibres and paper-waste. These are pre-moulded to fit the various sizes of basket. Circles are scored at intervals around the side of the liner, and you simply press on the scored areas to force away sections of the liner to create holes through which trailing plants can be inserted into the side of the basket. Although the theory is fine, in practice you can have holes only where the manufacturer lets you.

Another fibre-based idea has a disc with what appears to be a series of large petals radiating from it, rather like a stylized daisy. These can be folded to fit inside a range of different sized baskets. Loose fibres in the form of coir or coconut fibre are used to make a mat that can be pushed into the basket. These have the advantage that they are a bit like moss with a loose finish, which looks far more natural than the other manufactured types. The colouring in some types is even a greenish-brown, which makes the resemblance to moss even greater. They are biodegradable, so can go on the compost heap when you have finished with them.

In addition to simple sheets of polythene, you can use a fine-mesh polythene net. These can be purchased either in packs, which are manufactured specifically for the hanging basket trade, or, more cheaply, in lengths cut from a roll that is sold as greenhouse shading. The mesh is fine enough to hold in the compost but large enough to allow excess water to drain away.

Whichever liner you choose, it should not be too conspicuous, should allow you to plant through it and should not be too bulky. Moss is, despite all the alternatives now available, still the preferred method for many, but for cheapness, pieces of black polythene are perfectly acceptable, as long as they are hidden when the basket is full.

While it would be difficult to get away with a mixture of colours like this in a border, in a basket they create a glorious unselfconscious blaze.

Planting Styles

THERE ARE GOOD baskets, and there are bad baskets. Unfortunately, one too often sees the latter. Probably the single factor that makes a bad basket is the sight of an ugly liner, especially a piece of crumpled black polythene. Choose the right liner and fill the basket well with plants, and you are likely to succeed in producing an acceptable basket. However, to produce a really good display, it is worth thinking about the plants you are using and the image you want to create.

At first, it is difficult to visualize what the basket will be like when all you have before you are a few packets of seed or some small plants only a few centimetres high. As you plant

up more and more baskets, your eye will become adjusted and you will be able to look at an empty wire basket and imagine how it will be when it is full of colourful plants in the style you want. All that is needed is practice at creating baskets and a great deal of looking at other baskets as you go around other gardens or peep over garden fences.

The first thing is to consider the season for which you are making the basket. Because the size is so limited, there is no point in trying to make a basket that will last all year round, with a few plants for spring, a few for summer and so on. Stick to one season. If possible, select plants that all flower for the same length of time. This is not essential, of course, but the basket will look better if there are no dead patches where some plants have finished flowering. There is little point in choosing plants that flower for only a limited period unless they are likely to produce such a magnificent splash that it is worth replacing the whole basket once it is over.

In practice, this means that your choice is largely restricted to annual plants that tend to have a long flowering period. Perennial plants are more likely to come into flower for a fortnight and then pass over. Peonies, for example, are spectacular plants and very desirable to have in the garden, but they flower for only a brief period. Begonia flowers, on the other hand, which in some respects resemble peony flowers, can continue for months.

Another point worth remembering is that not all plants will grow in baskets. Peonies, for example, would not make good basket plants unless you managed to keep them in their

Colour combinations are an important aspect. Here, just the use of two contrasting colours, gold and blue, makes a good impact.

114

pot, and that would have to be a big one at that. Some perennials do make good basket plants, but again, annuals, which generally do not have time to put on a great deal of growth below ground in their short lives, are the best choice.

So far only flowers have been mentioned, but it must be remembered that foliage plays a major part in any aspect of garden design, and hanging baskets are no exception. Even though it is perhaps not as important as in other areas, foliage should never be neglected. At its simplest it forms a background against which the plants can be seen. Nasturtiums, for example, always look best against their own rich green foliage. Take away the leaves, and the bright red or orange flowers lose a lot of their impact. We should also consider adding plants solely for their foliage effect. This is particularly true of plants with a variegated foliage, such as the variegated ground ivy, *Glechoma hederacea* 'Variegata', or the similar looking plectranthus, *Plectranthus madagascariensis* 'Variegated Mintleaf'.

Foliage can be used to soften the effect of flowers – the soft grey or lime green helichrysum is good for this – or it may be used as a visual link across the design as long trails wind their way across the basket. The texture of the foliage is also important. The shiny leaves of ivy-leaved geraniums (*Pelargonium*), for example, will lighten an arrangement, while the duller texture of the leaves of zonal geraniums will have the opposite effect.

The final element in the range of plants that we can use is the actual shape of the plant. Some are stiff and upright, while others are lax and trailing. Some have wonderfully sweeping stems that are covered with airy flowers, while others are compact, sometimes almost dumpy, and create solid blocks of colour.

So our palette consists of flowering plants, preferably annuals with a long season, plants with good foliage that can vary in colour, shape or texture, and plants that have strong shapes to them. A quick glance through the baskets illustrated in this book will soon show you plenty of examples of each type.

It is now time to consider what we do with the plants. The first thing is to look at what factors influence the design and then how to get the structure and, finally, the colours right.

There are several ways of deciding what type of basket to create. The first is to look at the house or building on which you want to hang the basket and decide what would be the best type for the 'mood' of the building. You could choose a bright and cheerful display to cheer up a dull façade, or you could choose soft romantic colours that would fit in with the climbing roses around the door and the chintz curtains at the window. You might well choose something eye-catching to draw attention away from ugly brickwork or from a maze of drainpipes, or you might want something that will add to the overall picture without drawing too much attention to the basket itself.

The basket might reflect your own mood and personality. If you are an outward-going person you might like something bright that draws attention to itself, or perhaps you are a more romantic type. who would prefer to have soft colours and wispy trails. Alternatively, of course, you might simply design a basket to suit your own preferences. It may be that you like a particular style or that you like particular plants and dislike others. There is not much point in using masses of lobelia if you cannot stand the sight of the plant. On the other hand, if you love the way lobelia trails and pops up here and there throughout the basket, then why not use it?

A factor that often dominates the style of a basket but that you should really fight against because it so often produces mediocre results is when a basket is designed around the plants that are available. It may be that your local garden centre carries a very limited range or that you feel obliged to use plants grown by a relative or friend. If you can, resist this path and look further afield for your plants, or grow your own so that you can choose what you use.

Once you have decided on the style of basket you want – a bright, colourful arrangement, perhaps, or one filled with subtle colours and foliage – what is your next step? Colour theory frightens a lot of people, who may feel that because they have no artistic ability or training they will not be able to come to terms with it. However, most of us are quite happy to go out and choose the clothes we wear, making up different combinations for different occasions. We know how to dress formally and informally or how to match the colour of a sweater to that of a skirt or trousers, and we decorate our own homes, choosing paints, wallpapers, carpets and curtains that will combine to create the impression we want to convey. The same basic, often instinctive, feelings can be applied to the choice of colour combinations in the garden, or in this case to hanging baskets.

Hot bright colours are full of excitement and gaiety. Choose scarlets and oranges and golden-yellows to create this kind of feeling. These colours have immediate impact and draw the eye straight to them. A bright red in the middle of an otherwise subdued basket will catch the viewer's attention, while a whole basket of bright colours will pull the eye away from some ugly pipework or other unattractive features.

Hot colours advance and always seem closer than they are. Putting a basket containing bright red plants in the distance will have the effect of bringing it forwards. Hot colours are not only exciting, they are also welcoming, almost like a glowing fire on a cold day. They do well near entrances and against cold or harsh-coloured walls.

Cool and soft colours, such as the blues, are not as exciting. They are more romantic and can cool down a warm, sunny place. They do not draw attention to themselves in the same way as oranges and reds, but blend together to make a complete picture. Cool colours tend to recede into the distance, so that a basket of soft blues and violets will appear further away than it is. Do not hang them at a great height or they will not be noticed from a distance. However much you may like cool blues and variegated leaves, be careful how you use them: in bleak surroundings they may make the situation appear even bleaker.

Depending on the style of basket you are designing, you can decide that all the colours should be harmonious and work together to produce a sympathetic picture or you can choose plants that will clash and create some form of discord. The former scheme will have a calming effect while the latter will add a touch of excitement to the basket. Remember, though, that too much excitement can become boring, so decide carefully the effect you want create. Harmonious colours are those that sit next to each other on what artists and designers know as the colour wheel. For example, yellow and

orange work well together and tend to blend into a single picture, while yellow and blue stand out from one another and will break up the picture into separate elements. The general effect of the latter will be seen to be much crisper and almost refreshing. If this is beginning to sound complicated, think about it in terms of the colour combination of clothes and it should become much more straightforward.

In many respects, the simpler a basket the more effective it is. The use of too many colours or textures will make the basket seem very 'busy' and restless. On the other hand, limiting your plants to a single colour, or perhaps two colours, has a much more calming and restful effect. It must be remembered that a hanging basket is a relatively small area, and if you try to cram too much into it, it will look overcrowded with colour.

A small hanging basket can, however, act as a focal point. The eye is drawn towards it and takes it in at a glance. This limited area can, therefore, be made as gaudy as you like without the whole house or garden appearing in the same light. This is why baskets are so good for cheering up the scene: they can be as bright as you want and yet they do not take over the whole of your garden in the same way as, say, a large bed of bright annuals.

Having established that you are going to reflect your mood or the house's mood and having decided whether you want a bright display or something more discreet, you must now consider how you are going to arrange the basket. You can scatter the plants around the basket to get a dotted, busy effect or you can group them, perhaps using a strong colour in the centre, with contrasting or softer colours around it. Another possibility is to dot the plants around but to have a band of colour moving through it, perhaps diagonally like a stream or a waterfall. This can often be very effective.

A dotted effect is restless because there is nowhere for the eye to come to a halt, and such an arrangement often works well near a door or path, where there is constant coming and going. A plain basket, on the other hand, is very restful. Although no particular feature is prominent, the eye does not wander around but takes in the basket as a whole. Such baskets are restful and serene, but rarely of any great interest. Interest is generated by contrasting colours, shapes and textures. Place a strong colour in the middle or in a stream across the basket, and the eye has something to focus on or to follow. It then explores the surrounding colours, seeking out relationships. Unconsciously the viewer is looking at the whole basket and often enjoying what they see.

The style of the basket is likely to depend on the season. In the summer there is a tremendous range of plants available. Annuals in particular provide a very wide range of colours and textures and last for a very long period. Perennials can also be used but these tend to be less bright and can often be used for more elegant and sophisticated designs. At the end of summer, plants that take on autumnal colours can be used to give a seasonal flavour.

Winter is a difficult period. The usual standby is to use foliage plants, but a surprising number of plants that flower at that time of year can be used. Because baskets are usually hung next to walls, they benefit from any heat that is radiated from them, and this frequently brings plants, such as primulas, into flower long before they would in the open garden. In sheltered spots it is also possible to use plants such as the florist's cyclamen. These are tender but will survive if the basket is moved under cover during frosty spells.

As winter turns to spring there is an increasing number of plants in flower, many of them in the bright yellows, blues and reds that herald the change in the weather. This is a time for bright, cheerful baskets.

Look through the pictures in this book and choose the ones that you like best or the ones that you think would suit the proposed position best. Make them up and then look carefully at them and work out why you like them. Gradually you will begin to understand what you like and will be able to step out on your own and create your own designs. It is not a difficult or complicated process, but if you begin to get worried, forget all about style and design and just imagine that they are clothes you are choosing and you will be surprised how well you succeed.

Simplicity itself. A single plant (*Pelargonium* 'L'Elégance') with an interesting variegated foliage and pale flowers makes a wonderful basket.

117

Site and Situation

ON THE WHOLE siting is not a problem – most people know where they want to put their baskets before they even buy them. However, there are a few points to bear in mind.

Baskets need not be hung only on house walls or porches. There is a surprisingly large number of situations where they will make an effective contribution to the look of a place. On

the house itself, some of the best positions are near an entrance, either hanging on the wall near a door or on the porch if there is one. Try to balance the scene with a basket on each side of a door if there is room. On each side of a window or hanging from a balcony are other favourite positions. They can also be hung on blank walls to introduce some interest, but try to arrange them in a group or in a pattern and not to dot them at random or the overall effect will be spotty.

The same principle applies to hanging baskets on the walls of outbuildings. Choose their positions carefully and try not to dot them around. They can be useful for decorating ugly garages or sheds, when a colourful basket will often draw the eye away from a raw concrete wall. Baskets can also be hung on boundary walls and fences, but if they belong to neighbours, especially if it is the wall to their house, check first that they do not mind you fixing the supporting bracket to their property – it could prevent a lot of trouble later on.

Hanging baskets make attractive additions to archways, pergolas and even arbours. They help detract from the starkness of the woodwork or ironwork and add yet another vertical dimension to the garden. If the archways or pergolas are on a walkway, make sure that the baskets are either high enough for people to pass underneath them or are sited to one side.

You can fix baskets in arbours or pergolas constructed over paved areas where you relax and eat, and it is easy to change the baskets around to change the mood, using those with white or blue flowers in the evening, because these will show up in the dusk, while red or purple displays will be good during the daytime but will disappear with the fading light.

A series of hanging baskets in a border creates a mound of colour. Care must be taken not to overdo this effect.

This is also the place to use perfumed flowers. Mixing hanging baskets with hanging lanterns can also be extremely effective for after-dark evenings spent relaxing or entertaining outside.

Another marvellous way of using them is to hang them from posts. You can place a series of posts along a path and hang the baskets from cross pieces. These can be relatively low, so that you can look down on the baskets, or they can be at an old-fashioned street-light height so that they hang just above your head. You could, of course, hang them from the cross bars of street lamps. An alley of baskets along a path is certainly an attractive way to greet visitors.

One of the great things about hanging baskets is that they are mobile. You can easily take one down and re-hang it somewhere else or replace it with another. So that you are not stuck with a particular colour scheme, it is often a good idea to have a few baskets in reserve so that you can change the baskets around or change the effect in a particular area.

Hot, exciting colours go well with busy areas, where there is a lot of activity, and so they are ideal for a basket near an entrance. Hot or warm colours are also welcoming, which reinforces the idea of using them near doorways. Cool and soft colours, on the other hand, are more restrained and tend to slow down the action and encourage a feeling of relaxation. Try these more muted and harmonious colours near areas such as patios or arbours where you are likely to sit and relax.

One aspect of hanging baskets that is often forgotten is that it is possible to choose flowers that have a pleasant scent. Plants such as tobacco plants (*Nicotiana*) are wonderful for perfuming the evening air, and baskets containing them should be placed where the flowers' scents can waft into the house through open windows or doors. They can also be placed near where you might sit outside.

Herbs can be used to make a fascinating and useful hanging basket. They are not long-lived in the relatively small amount of compost that a basket contains, but they can easily be replaced. Hang a basket filled with herbs just outside the kitchen door where the cook can easily reach them.

Large, fulsome displays such as this should be sited where they will not be in the way.

It is essential to choose a site that is suitable for the flowers you are using, or, to put it another way, choose the plants for the site you will be using. Some plants need full sun all day. Others, such as busy lizzies and begonias, often prefer to avoid the sun for at least the hottest part of the day. There are not many plants that can be used on north-facing walls, although busy lizzies are a welcome exception. Most plants will, however, last for a while under such conditions, and you can always change the baskets around once a week if you are desperate to have colour in a sunless place.

On a practical level all baskets should be accessible. They must be watered and maintained regularly, so there is little point in having a basket that is well out of reach. If they are hung from balconies or next to windows, it is possible that they can be reached from inside the house. Elsewhere, you may have to get a ladder once a day for watering, which can become a terrible chore, particularly if you do not like ladders or if the ground beneath the basket is uneven. Watering can be facilitated by using a pump-action system, which will allow you to reach some distance above your head, but for the perfect basket you will still need access for deadheading.

One way to cope with this is to use some form of pulley system, but then you must be prepared to have ugly ropes to raise and lower the basket. As already noted, there is a special system on the market that includes a counterbalanced spring, which allows you to pull the basket down with a pole and then push it back up again when you have finished attending to it. It is a discreet device, which looks no more cumbersome than a pulley block but has none of the ropes involved with that system.

Another practical consideration is weight. On the whole most baskets are not very heavy, but they are still dangerous objects to have hanging around above people's heads. It is your responsibility to make sure that they are well secured and preferably sited away from where people walk.

It is not always possible to avoid wind on the side of a building, but wherever possible choose the calmest position for a basket. Certainly, if you are creating large, frothy displays

Hanging baskets near windows means that they provide colour and interest both from without and within the house.

with plenty of spreading stems, you will need to find a windless situation or the basket will be spoilt by the first gust. Another problem with constant wind is that the basket will grow unevenly, with not much growth or flowers on the windward side and a disproportionate amount on the other. If you live in a windy area – near the sea, perhaps – or in a permanent draught caused by tall adjacent buildings, think carefully about your displays. It will be better to create those that use plants that are tight growing rather than extending out in long, arching stems. Keep the arrangement compact and you will be able to make a credible display. It may be possible to grow a shrub or group of shrubs on the windward side of where you want to hang baskets to create a windbreak, or you could use trellising, fixed at right angles to the wall and covered with climbers, to get the same effect.

A minor but very irritating problem with a windy site, especially at night, is the sound of a basket constantly swinging to and fro. If this is likely to happen, fix the basket in a way that it does not squeak, creak, groan, rattle or make one of those sleep-reducing sounds that most people find hard to endure.

One of the problems of using half-baskets is that they are usually attached direct to the wall. This means that excess water is likely to trickle out of the basket and down the wall. In many cases this may not matter, but in some situations the water and odd bits of compost and fertilizers may well stain the wall, which is particularly likely to be the case with painted walls, especially white. Another, more serious, aspect of this problem occurs if you have an older house without cavity walls. Constant water draining out of the basket is likely to sink into the brickwork and cause a damp patch and may even stain on the inside of the wall. So think carefully before you use them. You could use a solid container rather than a basket, but, if the plants are to grow properly, even these should have drainage holes. Hanging baskets are not a problem because they should always be hung clear of the wall, with any water dripping straight to the ground.

While on the question of excess water, remember that not many passers-by will appreciate water dripping on their heads. You need to take this into consideration when you are positioning your baskets.

Planting and Maintenance

THE GREAT JOY of hanging baskets is that you can put on a magnificent display with little effort or cost. Baskets are easy to create and to look after, although, as with all aspects of gardening, you get nothing for free, and you have to do a bit of work in the form of watering and simple deadheading. Another advantage is that little space and few facilities are required to produce a basket. You can, of course, get really involved with the whole operation and grow all your own plants, in which case the process become a little more complicated, but even then, with the use of window-sills and balconies, you do not need a garden. The initial costs are low, with the baskets costing little, and the running costs are not much more, especially if you grow all your own plants from seed or cuttings.

OBTAINING PLANTS

Most gardeners approach planting a hanging basket in one of two ways. One group go to their local garden centre and buy a mass of plants and then set about using them in the most attractive way that they can. The second group plan the design of the baskets and then go out and buy the plants they need to fulfil that design. Both methods have their advocates, but the latter, using the principles laid down in the earlier chapter on style, is to be preferred if you want to achieve the best baskets.

Before you set out to buy plants or seeds, make a shopping list of the plants you want. You will get ideas from looking at other baskets, both in reality and in books. Note those plants that you find particularly attractive and want to grow, and then, with this list by your side, decide on the design of the basket and how many of each plant you will need.

Alternatively, choose one of the recipes in this book and make a note of the ingredients.

Once you have decided on the plants you want, you have two alternatives: to buy them or to grow them from seed. There is a wide range of garden centres and nurseries or, in some areas, you can buy them from the roadside. They may be plants that have been produced by good gardeners who are selling off surplus stock or they may be being sold by a farm shop or some other outlet that has not got experience in looking after plants and the results may be disappointing. Choose with care.

The disadvantage of buying from a garden centre or nursery is that you might not find the range of plants you require. There may be a selection of petunias, but only bedding forms and not the trailing varieties you want. There may be mixed boxes of seedlings that are not yet showing their colour, while you want only white ones. The great advantage of growing your own is that you can choose the colours and the type of plant that you need. A glance through the catalogues of the major seed merchants will show the vast range available – for example, there are a number of different forms of white petunias to choose from.

When you are buying from a nursery or garden centre, always choose plants that are free from pests and diseases. Reject any that look drawn or sickly, particularly when plants are sold in blocks, because it means that a large number have been grown in inadequate space. Plants in individual pots will always be better than overcrowded ones. Avoid plants that are already in flower because these often do not develop properly and will probably stop flowering soon after you get them home. If you have nowhere to store plants against late frosts, do not buy them too early.

Growing plants from seed is not difficult, and although it helps if you have a greenhouse or a cold frame, they can easily be produced on the kitchen window-sill. The only thing to remember is to start early in the year so that the plants are ready when you want to plant them out.

Some plants can be used every year. Trailing ivies, for example, can be kept going and have the advantage of being mature when you want to use them, while newly bought ones may take the whole season to fulfil their promise.

PLANTING

You do not need green fingers to make a hanging basket, but there are a few guidelines that will help you on your way.

Remember that many of the plants that you are likely to use in your basket are tender and should not, therefore, be put outside until the risk of frost has passed. If you have a greenhouse or conservatory, you can prepare the basket in advance and keep it hanging inside until the early summer. By then the plants will have matured and the whole basket should already be in flower. If you have to plant up just before you hang the basket in early summer, it will, obviously, take longer for the plants to come into flower and for the basket to reach its full potential.

Working on a round-bottomed basket is not easy, and there are two solutions. The first is to hang the basket in the greenhouse or wherever you are working so that it is at a convenient height for planting. The second is to balance the basket on a large flowerpot or bucket. This method is not as satisfactory if you are using trailing plants that are already well developed. Another point to consider is that if you are not particularly strong and have nobody to help, you may well be better off hanging the basket in its final position before you fill or it might be too heavy to move. This does, of course, assume that the basket is not too high from the ground.

The first task is to insert the liner. This is not usually difficult, but you should remember to trim off any excess that

Baskets containing tender annuals like these can be made in advance and kept under glass so that they are already in bloom when hung out.

123

sticks up above the rim of the basket. If you are using moss it can be difficult to keep it in place if you line the whole basket in one go. It is easier if you line the bottom and partway up the side and then add some compost to hold it in place, before adding more moss and more compost, and so on. When they use moss, some gardeners like to use an inner plastic liner to prevent the compost getting washed though the moss. Use perforated plastic for this so that the moss stays moist.

There are several composts to choose from. My own preference is for soil-based composts, often referred to as John Innes composts, which are heavier than soil-less (sometimes referred to as peat-based) composts but which do not dry out as easily and which, if they do, can more easily be re-wetted. Many of the soil-less composts are almost impossible to re-soak once they have dried out – the water just runs down the sides of the container. However, the choice of composts is a personal one and you should use whichever you prefer. An advantage of soil-less composts is that their lightness makes life easier when you come to lift the basket into position.

Because a basket contains a small amount of compost relative to the number of plants planted in it, it is important that it is kept well watered and fed. In hot weather, as we shall see, the basket is likely to need watering at least once a day and often more frequently than this. To help overcome this, manufacturers have produced water-retaining granules, which absorb water and store it until the roots of the plants need it, when it is released. These granules do work, but such is the plants' demand for moisture that you will still have to water regularly – once a day in hot weather and once every two days in more overcast conditions. The granules are simply mixed into the compost, usually in the lower part where the plants' roots are located.

Another additive is fertilizer. The traditional way to feed plants is by adding a liquid feed to at least one watering a week. The modern alternative is to use a slow-release fertilizer, which slowly lets out chemicals so that they last a whole season without having the need for a liquid feed. These fertilizers are available in two forms. Granules are simply mixed into the compost or a larger, tablet can be pressed into the surface of the compost when the basket is complete.

When you have lined your basket, selected the compost and decided if you are going to use water-retaining granules and a slow-release fertilizer, the next task is to fill the basket with compost. Do this by filling it between two-thirds and three-quarters full with compost, adding the water-retaining and fertilizer granules if you are using them and mixing them all together. Follow the manufacturer's recommendations on the container for the appropriate quantities of water-retaining and slow-release fertilizer granules to use. Fill up the rest of the basket with compost alone and lightly firm it down. It is now ready to plant.

If you are proposing to insert plants through the liner in the side of the basket, the procedure is slightly different. Start by partly filling the basket with compost and mix in any granules you want to use. Next, make holes through the liner in the required positions. Slits in a polythene liner are usually sufficient, although if you are using a pre-moulded liner you need to press out the pre-formed holes. Gently push the roots of each plant through the hole and pull the compost around them. After putting in all the plants around the side, continue to fill the basket with compost, firming it down around their roots.

Now it is time to plant the top of the basket. If you can easily move around the basket or turn it around, start planting in the middle and work outwards. If you can only approach it easily from one direction, start at the back and move forwards. Dig holes with your fingers as required, and keep the surface of the compost just below the rim of the basket. The plants should be at the same depth as they were in their original pots.

Some gardeners prefer to start planting when the basket is only part filled. They position the plants and then pour more compost around them. This is not always as easy as it sounds, however, because the basket is likely to be rather full of plants and it is not always possible to ensure that they are the correct distance apart as you try to add the compost.

Once they are all in position, gently firm down the compost with your hands and level it off. This is the moment to insert the slow-release fertilizer tablet if you are using one.

The basket should now be thoroughly watered. The best way to do this, provided you have not got a lot of trailing plants or plants in the side of the basket, is to stand it in a bowl or bucket of water. Remember that when it has soaked its fill, it will be very heavy. Stand it on an empty bucket so that the excess water can drain away. If there are too many trailing plants to make this an easy option, water from above using a watering can.

When the water has stopped dripping out it is time to hang the basket. You may need help to do this, especially if it is fairly large. Always get help if you are unsure if you can manage it yourself. There is little point in putting yourself into hospital, leaving others to enjoy your work.

If there is still a likelihood of frosts, the basket can be left in the greenhouse or conservatory where the plants will continue to grow, but do not hang them in a dark or shady corner, or they will become horribly drawn.

Half-baskets that are screwed to the wall need to filled *in situ,* but the same procedure is followed. Those that are suspended with hooks can be hung up in the greenhouse on the edge of the bench or propped up against a box and worked on in the normal way.

MAINTENANCE

Although hanging baskets are virtually trouble-free, they still need a bit of attention. Undoubtedly the most arduous task is watering, which is something that must be carried out every day, unless nature does it for you, and it rains.

A colourful display like this will soon look tired and tatty unless you deadhead and remove dead items.

Of course, the main problem with watering hanging baskets is that it is not easy to reach them with a watering can, particularly if they are well above your head. If you are not using a pulley arrangement or counterbalanced spring, you will need to use steps or a ladder, which can be difficult, because a watering can full of water is heavy. If your baskets are situated near windows or hanging from balconies, they can be watered from above in the normal way.

One possible solution to the problem of raising water to a high basket is to attach a hose pipe to a pole or broomstick. Take care, however, because if the water pressure is too high, not only could it damage the plants or even wash them out of the compost, it could also deluge the gardener beneath. A simpler alternative is to buy one of the watering systems designed especially for hanging baskets. This consists of a closed container with a long tube emerging from it with a hook on the end. You can deliver a controlled amount of water in a gentle stream well above your head safely and with little effort. They are certainly to be recommended if you want to water high-up baskets.

Never let the baskets dry out: as soon as you see the petunias beginning to wilt, it is time to give the plants more water. On the other hand, be careful not to over-water. The compost should be moist but not sodden, or the plants may rot. If the compost is particularly fibrous, add some grit or sharp sand to it to improve its drainage.

Winter baskets do not need anything like as much water as summer ones. Very few plants are in full growth at that time of year and their take-up of moisture is limited. The baskets should be kept moist but certainly never over-watered. There is often sufficient natural water in the form of rain, but even in winter there can be sunny, dry spells during which baskets can dry out remarkably quickly. There is, however, no need to add either water-retaining granules or slow-release fertilizer in winter baskets.

Do not forget that if you go away on holiday you must arrange for someone to water the plants for you, or they will not be there when you get back.

If you have used a slow-release fertilizer, in either granule or tablet form, there is no need to feed the plants. However, if you do not use this method then it is important that you add a liquid feed to one watering each week. Check the manufacturer's guidelines for the quantity to add to your watering can. Because plant growth is slow in the winter and fewer nutrients are required, feed winter baskets only about once a month.

In addition to watering and feeding your hanging baskets, there is one more important task if you want to have perfect displays. You must remove all dead flowerheads as they occur, because dead and mouldy petals soon make a basket look untidy. You must also remove any stems that have finished flowering and cut back those stems that become too long and straggly. Many plants will send out new shoots from the base when they are cut back.

If plants exhaust themselves and stop flowering, they can often be simply removed and replaced by fresh ones. It is often a good idea, especially if you grow your own plants, to keep a few spares so that you can freshen up a flagging basket.

Most beginners dread pests and diseases, but, in fact, these are generally not too much of a problem. Most baskets last for only a relatively short period, and there is little time for either pests or diseases to develop to serious proportions. Slugs cannot fly, and the most serious problem is likely to be greenfly. If they do become a nuisance, you can either use an insecticidal spray or you can scrap the basket altogether. If you use chemicals, always follow the instructions on the container and only spray those parts of the plant that are infected. Spray in the evening, when beneficial insects will not be harmed.

The great thing about hanging baskets is that you start again from scratch each year, so if you do get a problem of some sort, rather than trying to get rid of it, which may be expensive and messy, leaving you with an unbalanced or tatty basket, you can simply discard the whole arrangement and start again if there is time or pack the basket away until the next season. Unlike the main garden, where you may want to protect a tree or valuable plant, the contents of most baskets are wholly expendable.

At the end of the season or once the plants begin to look tired, empty the contents of the basket onto the compost heap, clean the basket and put it away for next year, when you can start all over again.

Index

PHOTOGRAPH ACKNOWLEDGMENTS

John Fielding 20, 118, 125; **John Glover** 6, 7, 9, 11, 13, 17, 19, 27, 31, 97, 99, 101, 103, 109, 120, 123; **Jerry Harpur** 15 (Bourton House, Glos), 49, 51 (White Hart Royal Hotel, Glos), 55 (Brenda Harding, Oxon), 57 (White Hart Royal Hotel, Glos), 59, 61, 63, 65, 69, 71 (White Hart Royal Hotel, Glos), 73 (Bourton House, Glos), 75 (White Hart Royal Hotel, Glos), 105 (Pimlico Flowers, London), 108 (Bourton House, Glos); **Marcus Harpur** 43 (RHS Chelsea, 1995), 45 (RHS Chelsea, 1995), 53 (Dr Mary Harpur), 67 (RHS Chelsea, 1995), 114 (Dr Mary Harpur); **Andrew Lawson** 21, 23, 25 (Carolyn McNab, Oxon), 29 (Bourton House, Glos), 33, 35, 37, 39, 41, 95, 107 (Joe Elliott, Glos), 113 (W.E. Turville, Ilmington, Warwicks), 117, 119; **Clive Nichols** 83, 85 (Greenhurst Garden Sussex/Designer: Gilly Hopton), 87, 89, 111, 112 (Bourton House, Glos); **Photos Horticultural** 77, 81, 91, 93, 110 (Webbs of Wynchbold); **Steve Wooster** 79.